THE SCIENCE
OF MONEY

THE SCIENCE OF MONEY

How to Increase your Income and Become Wealthy

BRIAN TRACY
with DAN STRUTZEL

gildanpress

gildanpress

Published 2017 by Gildan Press
an imprint of Gildan Media LLC.

Distributed through the Book market by Hachette Book Group, USA

First Edition: 2017

Front Cover design by David Rheinhardt of Pyrographx

Interior design by Meghan Day Healey of Story Horse, LLC.

Library of Congress Cataloging-in-Publication Data
is available upon request

ISBN: 978-1-469-00538-6

Manufactured in the United States of America by LSC Communications

10 9 8 7 6 5 4 3 2 1

CONTENTS

FOREWORD   vii

INTRODUCTION   ix

ONE   What Is Money?   1

TWO   The Myths about Money   32

THREE   The Science of Spending   68

FOUR   The Science of Debt   85

FIVE   The Science of Generating Income   108

SIX   The Science of Creating Wealth   135

SEVEN   The Science of Multiplying Wealth   156

EIGHT   The Science of Wealth Protection   172

NINE   The Science of Money and Happiness   187

TEN   The Science of Economics: Rules for a Vibrant National Economy   203

INDEX   235

FOREWORD

The Dynamic Conversations Series

Brian Tracy is one of the world's foremost authorities on business and personal success. He has given more than 5000 talks and seminars to over 5 million people and is a business coach to top leaders in major industries worldwide.

Dan Strutzel is a 25-year veteran of the personal development industry, publishing some of the most successful audio programs in history. He has worked up close and personally with most of the top personal development authors and speakers.

Dan was thrilled when Brian agreed to sit down together to discuss his seminar *The Science of Money: The Science of Happiness*. Meeting over the course of a long weekend, these thinkers were able to explore this topic deeply and at great length. These in-depth interviews were taped and are presented here. We hope you enjoy and benefit from their discussion.

INTRODUCTION

Dan Strutzel

Money remains one of the most thought-provoking, emotional, and polarizing subjects in the world. Scores of books, articles, blog posts, and speeches have been written on what money is, how to earn it, how to spend it, who has it and who does not, and a myriad of other topics. And yet, despite the constant focus on the topic, there is one word that describes the average person's views about money: *confusion.*

Despite some of the truly great research that has been published on the topic, there is so much misinformation—what we might call financial white noise—about money that most people either rely on chance for their fortune or ignore the subject altogether. This is not only unnecessary, it is a tragedy. It's a tragedy because of the untapped human potential that is never uncovered when people leave their lives to chance, or worse, give up on their dreams. It's also totally unnecessary, because the secrets of money, how to create it, how to invest it, and how to spend it wisely, *are known.*

Truly, there is a Science of Money, just as there are sciences of nutrition, anatomy, astronomy, chemistry, and engineering. This

Science of Money has been tested and proven again and again, not just for years or for decades, but for millennia. While new theories of money can arise all the time—just as we have new theories for cures for cancer or baldness—the discipline of science and its rules for testing and verifying results will, in short order, move these ideas from the realm of theory to one of two categories: one, a verifiable fact, what Brian calls a *law*; or two, a disproven idea, what Brian calls a *myth*.

In this book, we will be examining both of these categories: the *laws* of money, which have been proven and can be relied upon as much as you can rely upon the sun rising in the east; and the *myths* of money. Myths can include those ideas that can exist without any basis, but may still survive as rumors; and also those ideas which claim to be true but which have been tested and disproven, or which, at best, have never been decidedly proven.

Ultimately, we have one central goal: to end the confusion around the topic, once and for all, and to present, in one, comprehensive place, the essential truths about money. If you simply study the ideas here and apply them to your life and your business, you will become financially successful, as surely as the sun will rise tomorrow.

ONE

What is Money?

In any scientific discipline, we need to define terms in order to be certain that we agree about the topic we are studying and about the ground rules for testing any theory about it. In this session, Brian will help to define the terms surrounding money. Some of his responses may surprise you.

Dan

Brian, let's begin by describing what we mean by the Science of Money and how money has been studied. Let's see how this study has produced many solid and reliable laws about how money can be earned or created, and how this flies in the face of many of the mystical and/or speculative theories out there.

Brian

If you want to get right down to the nitty-gritty, you start with the first law, which is called the *law of exchange*. It says that money is the medium through which people exchange their goods and services. They exchange their labor in the production of goods and services for the goods and services of others. Money is a medium of exchange for labor.

Before there was money, there was barter. This goes right back to 100,000 years ago, where someone would make a flint spearhead or a pot and exchange it for a carpet or a skin. In barter, people exchanged goods and services directly for goods and services without the medium of money. Then civilization grew, and barter became too clumsy. People found that they could exchange their goods and services for a medium like gold, silver, coins, seashells, wampum in early America—something that was scarce and valuable. People would have a coin or something of value, which they could then exchange for a chicken or a goat or something else. It makes the whole process more efficient.

That was the beginning of money, and it still defines what money is today, even though many people are very confused about it. It makes the whole process of exchange more efficient. Today we go to work and we exchange our work for money, which we then use to purchase the products of the work of other people. Basically money is the medium through which we exchange our work for the work of others.

The first corollary of this law of exchange is that money is a measure of the value that people place on goods and services. It's only what a person will pay that determines the value of something. Things do not have value in and of themselves; the value of a thing is only what somebody is willing to pay for it.

You can't say that your product or service is worth a given amount unless somebody else validates it by actually offering you that amount of money. Goods and services have no value apart from what someone is willing to pay for them. All value is therefore subjective. This is the basis of thought for the Austrian school, which is the best and most insightful school of economics in human history. It's based on the thoughts, feelings, attitudes, and opinions of the prospective purchaser at the moment of the buying decision.

The second corollary of this law of exchange says that your labor is viewed as a factor of production, that is, as a cost, by others. This demolishes almost all of the economic arguments about whether people should be paid $15 an hour or something else. One name for human beings is *homo economicus*. This means that we always act economically: we always try to get the very most for the very least. This is genetic; it's built into our DNA. It has never been otherwise in all of human history. We never will pay more if we can possibly pay less.

Each of us has a tendency to look upon the sweat of our brow as something special, because it's so intensely personal. It comes from us. It's an expression of who we are as persons. It's very emotional, as a matter of fact, because it's our life. But as far as others are concerned, our labor is just a cost. As intelligent consumers or as employers or customers, we want the very most for the very least, no matter whose labor is involved. This is why people manufacture in China or Taiwan or Vietnam or Indonesia: because the customer in America does not care where the product comes from. The customer simply cares about getting the very lowest price.

People talk about offshoring and sending jobs overseas and so on. It's not the companies; it's the customers that are demanding that they send these jobs there, because the products and services can be produced at a lower cost. Almost all of Apple's products are made in China. Why? It's because the cost to manufacture them in a more developed country is three or four times the amount it costs in China, so the customers in developed countries will not pay that amount. They demand—indirectly—that companies offshore these jobs so that they can have the very most for the very least.

For this reason, you can't place an objective value on your own labor, protesting and demanding increases and so on. It's only what other people are willing to pay for your labor in a competitive market that determines what you earn and what you are worth on financial terms. We'll talk later about the 99% versus the 1% and so on.

The third corollary of this law says the amount of money you earn is a measure of the value that others place on your contribution. In other words, it's the customers in the marketplace who determine what we're worth. It's the customers of the companies that we work for who determine what they will pay for the products and services we contribute to the production. That is what determines how much we will be paid. How much you are paid will be in direct proportion to the quantity and quality of your contribution in comparison with the contributions of others, combined with the value that other people place on your contributions.

One thing I used to say is that you are competing every single day with every other person in your company. People would get really huffy about that; they'd say, "We don't compete, we all work together as team members." The fact is that the person who determines your paycheck determines how much you will be paid in comparison with how much other people are paid. That's why most companies have a rule that you're not allowed to discuss your pay with other people, because your pay is determined by what the company thinks you are worth relative to everyone else working around you.

The fourth corollary of the law of exchange is that money is an effect, not a cause. Your work or contribution to the value of a product or service is the cause, and the wage, salary, or earnings that you receive are the effect. If you wish to increase the effect, you have to increase the cause. Just as author Earl Nightingale said years ago, the law of cause and effect is the foundational law of all of human life, all of science, all technology, all mathematics, all money.

The fifth corollary of the law of exchange is that to increase the amount of money you are getting out, you must increase the value of the work that you are putting in. This is a phenomenal thing. People think that they can get more out without putting more in. They think this all over the world. You say, "Well, where's the money going to come from?" Their answer is, "Somewhere." If you press them on that, they say, "Well, the money should come from other people who are creating more value, who therefore are earning more. Then they should give it to me—even though, according to the market, I'm creating less value—so that I don't feel bad." This kind of subjective attitude—that I'm entitled to more money—is absolute nonsense. That's why it leads to riots and strikes and everything else.

We say to earn more money, you must add more value. If you look at business, the secret to wealth creation, which we'll talk about later, is to add value. Sometimes I ask people how many of them work on straight commission. I'll ask 1000 people, and about 10% or 15% of people will raise their hands. The truth of the matter is, *everybody* works on straight commission. What does that mean? It means everybody gets a percentage of the value that they create. If you're not happy with the percentage that you're getting, create more value, become worth more so that your boss or your customers will willingly pay you more money because they value your contribution so much.

Some people earn $10 an hour; some people earn $1000 an hour. I have a friend who upgraded his skills from being a commercial lawyer to being a lawyer in intellectual copyright, a field nobody was in. It was a white space. Companies like Sony and Disney and the biggest companies in the world eagerly pay him $1000 an hour to help them with intellectual property law, because the amounts involved are hundreds of millions of dollars, and he's an expert. He made himself so valuable that they get in line to pay him whatever he wants. He is often paid $2 million or $3 million to vet a single contract or merger between companies that have intellectual property, such as movie companies.

To earn more money, you must add more value, so you must increase your knowledge. As management expert Peter Drucker said, we're all knowledge workers, so by increasing your amount of knowledge about how to do your business better, you increase your value, and people will be willing and eager to thrust money into your hand. Or you increase your skill level so that you can get more and better work done in the same period of time. Or you improve your work habits so that you're far more productive.

The highest-paid people in every society and every business are always described as being very result-oriented. They are highly productive. I have worked with people and just taught them time management skills, and they've tripled their income in less than a year doing the same job for the same company. The company willingly gives them more money because they're producing vastly more value. Everybody works on straight commission.

Or you can work longer and harder hours. The most successful people always work much harder than others. In fact, statistics say that about fifty-nine to sixty hours a week puts you in the top 20%. If you work seventy hours a week, you'll be in the top 5% or 10%. The average person today works a forty-hour week, but according to the labor studies, during that week he or she only works thirty-two hours. Why? It's because they take coffee breaks and lunches and start earlier and stop later. In those thirty-two hours, they waste 50% of that time, mostly with idle chitchat, Facebook, social media, Internet, phoning friends, and so on. So the average person is only doing sixteen hours of productive work each week, and in that time they do work of low value. Then they don't understand why they don't get paid more money.

The one secret to success is to work all the time you work. Start earlier, work harder, stay later, and work the whole darned time. Don't mess around. Don't chat with your friends. Don't go out for lunch or coffee or read the paper or surf the Internet. When you come to work, work. Put your head down full blast and work.

You can also work more creatively, or you can do anything that enables you to get greater leverage and results from your efforts. Some people produce five times as much as other people in the same eight hours a day.

By the way, all wealthy people work six days a week. This comes in study after study after study. It's not hard to work six days a week. If you're doing work that you really enjoy and you're doing it really well and you're getting great results, you get pumped up. It makes you happy. In fact, successful people have to use self-discipline to *not* work because they like their work so much.

One of your great responsibilities, which we will talk about later, is for you to find work that you enjoy so much that it gives you energy and you have to force yourself to stop. For people who are doing the right work, time stands still. They forget to eat.

They forget to take breaks. They forget to go for coffee. They're so engrossed in their work that they have to be torn away to eat or do something else.

The highest-paid people in our society are those who are continually improving in these areas to add greater value to the work that they're doing. This is the truth: the amount you earn is a direct reflection of the value that you create to improve the life and work of other people. All success in life comes from serving other people in some way. If you want to make a lot of money, serve a lot of people, and serve them in a way that really makes a difference to them.

Dan

Let's get some elaboration on that. Let's talk about people's pushback. To your point about adding value, you often hear people who are pushing for higher wages saying, "Look at the top executives. They get golden parachutes as they leave, even though the company lost money. Or look at the stock market. There are those who use the market like a casino. They roll the dice and make money when the stock market goes down or up."

People might say there are some distortions in the economy, so that it's not just a matter of value exchange. Talk about some of the objections that people throw up that are more cynical about the idea of adding value. How you would respond to them?

Brian

Let me tell you a famous story about what is called the *cargo cult*. During the Second World War, in New Guinea, the Allies came in, built airfields, and set up military bases to counter the Japanese. Some of the most vicious fighting went on in one half of New Guinea, and the other half was controlled by the Australians and Americans. All of their ammunition, food, supplies, everything, came in by these planes.

The Army Corps of Engineers would come in, unload the bulldozers, build the airstrips, and then they'd start bringing in all the food, clothing, everything, for the battle. When the war was over, they withdrew, and New Guinea went back to the jungle. The natives who were surrounding these areas and were used as workers during World War II had no idea where the wealth came from. They believed that wealth came from the cargo planes.

They started a cargo cult. They would build little dolls and little models of planes, and they would put them on little altars. They would light incense, and they would pray to them, worship them, and sing. They would pray for the planes to come back with the wealth inside.

The upshot of that story is that most people are abysmally ignorant about money, so they have the same sort of ideas. They believe in absolutely fantastical things.

When a person is lured away to take a job in a Fortune 500 company, they are offered very high pay, very high stock options, and their lawyers negotiate these contracts. I know this very well from my own experience. They negotiate severance pay. If something doesn't work out, if the company, after having decided to hire you, decides that they don't want you anymore—for any reason: the market turns down, you don't do a good job—they pay you severance. The severance pay is contractual.

They say, "Oh, these people get golden parachutes." Yes, those are the terms under which they took the job, and they took the job coming from somewhere else where they also had a fantastic job. This was just a normal part of it.

With regard to stock market speculation, you will find that the highest-paid people who work in the stock market work hard for that highest pay. For example, Warren Buffett, the billionaire, spends 80% of his time every single day studying the stock market, studying companies, studying the changes and changing fortunes in competition—80% of every day. He's eighty-four years old. He goes to work, he puts his head down, and he studies these investments.

He started off with $2000, and he used what is called the *value investing model*, which we will talk about later. He studies the value, the inherent value, of the company's products, services, management, and positioning in the industry compared to competition, national and international. So many things go into it. People who jump in and out of the stock market—most of them end up broke. It's like the professional poker players that go off to Las Vegas to make a lot of money. They find that they would earn as much if they had a laboring job at the end of the day because with the amount they win and the amount they lose, they make a few dollars an hour sitting there at the poker tables for twelve or fourteen hours. I just came from Las Vegas two days ago, and everybody there knows that stuff.

The people in the stock market, what they call the day traders, and now the flash traders, who are in and out and in and out—70% of them eventually are wiped out.

I just came back from meeting with one of my clients. He introduced me to a man who had spent several hundred million dollars developing a fifty-person flash trading organization. I saw it: huge screens, brilliant mathematicians day trading in and out of stocks, trying to get fractions of pennies here and there. He put in several hundred million dollars, and he lost it all. At the end of the day all these people working full-time sixteen hours a day lost everything and just walked away. Fortunately, he was a multibillionaire, so he could afford to lose several hundred million dollars on something speculative.

The fact of the matter is most people who make money in stocks are long-term players. Warren Buffett buys a stock and doesn't sell it for fifty years. He's a value trader. Every so often he will sell part of a holding, but usually to raise cash to purchase something else that is getting a better return at this point.

Today presidents of the Fortune 500 are earning an average of 303 times the average pay of the people who work in their corporations. Now the interesting thing is that they all started off at the original starting line, like marathon runners, at the beginnings of their careers. At the beginning of their careers, they were the same as everybody else. They started off in their jobs. They were put into pools or cubicles. Some of them had good educations. Some of them had average educations. Some of them had gotten straight A's. Some of them hadn't. Some of them came from good homes, some from poor homes. Some were Mayflower descendants and some were new immigrants that didn't speak the language when they started. Today they earn 303 times the pay of the average worker. That's about $10.3 million in annual salary, while the average person in their companies makes $52,000.

How could that be? They went back and traced it, and found there was one strategy. This is one of the great breakthroughs with regard to money. The strategy was that from the beginning of their careers, they asked this question: what one skill would help me to make a more valuable contribution now at this point in my career? They would go to their boss, and the boss would say, "If you were really good at marketing, or reading financial statements, or doing presentations, or building teams, or negotiating, then you could be really more valuable in your job."

These people would set that as a project, and put together a learning plan like going to school. They would find out the best books to read, the best audio programs to listen to (preferably ours), the best courses to take, and the best things to do every day to develop these skills. After a month or six months or a year, they would develop the skill, because all business skills are learnable.

The magic number is ten hours a week. While their friends were out socializing and chasing boys or girls and so on, these people would spend an average of two hours per day, five days per week, upgrading their skills. It became as natural to them as breathing in and breathing out. They came home at night, they had dinner with their spouses and children, and they studied two hours per night, five days a week.

I was in India the other day speaking. I said, "I'm not that familiar with your time zones, but how many hours are there in an average week here in India?" They all laughed at me. I said, "Yeah, it's 168 hours, seven times twenty-four." It's the same everywhere. Could you carve off ten hours per week to become one of the wealthiest, highest-paid, most respected people in your industry? They said, "Yes, of course you can." So really it's not a matter of ten hours out of 168. It's just simply a matter of willpower and self-discipline.

And each new skill is subject to the law of compounding. With each new skill, you can use your other skills at a higher level. You can increase your earning ability, your ability to make a contribution. You can be worth more because you can get better results.

You become more valuable, so people will pay you more and promote you faster.

The cumulative effect is like an avalanche. After ten or twenty or thirty years, you're in your forties and fifties, and you're earning 303 times the average of these other people who have not raised a finger to learn a thing since they took their first job. How come these people are paid so much? Some say, "They're just lucky." But these people make decisions that affect hundreds of millions of dollars, sometimes billions of dollars. They can make a decision to go in and out of an industry, to sell off a division or an entire series of factories, and the impact of that on the bottom line may be $1 billion. What do they get? They get $10 million. They get a fraction of 1% of the total economic impact of their decisions. But they started off working alone with a small assignment in a cubicle and with a little laptop. Now they're running huge businesses, and their offices take up the top floors of the best office buildings.

Everybody had the ability to do that, and everybody still has the ability to do something similar.

Dan

Would you tell a story about your own journey from someone with very modest means to someone who's achieved great wealth?

Brian

People often ask, what was your great motivation or your dream or your passion when you started? My answer was, to eat. What I wanted to do when I took my first job was make enough money to eat. My first job was washing dishes. I lived in a one-room apartment that had a stovetop on top, a refrigerator down below, a bathroom with a cheap shower, and a bed. That's where I lived. Those were my living quarters in different places for quite a while, because I was a laborer and I couldn't afford any more than that. I drove an old car. I wore old clothes. I worked eight to ten hours a day, and all I thought about was survival.

I had a couple of good experiences. When I was a young man, I found that I could get jobs in the neighborhood—I was twelve years old—cutting the grass, mowing lawns of other people. My parents eventually encouraged me to get a gas lawnmower. I did. They took me down to Sears, and they got me an absolutely dreadful lawnmower, because they didn't know anything about it. I would push this lawnmower around the neighborhood and mow lawns.

Pretty soon I was doing really well, and I decided to get a better lawnmower. I began to hang around a lawnmower shop. I looked at the lawnmowers they had, new and used and so on. I bought a used commercial lawnmower that was fabulous. It was the same kind of lawnmower they used to do golf greens. It was beautiful, and it threw the grass forward so it left no marks on the lawn.

Then I began to mow even more lawns. People began to recommend me because their lawns looked absolutely beautiful. Then I got a trimmer to do sidewalks and the flowerbeds and so on. Then I got a little cart to pull it around on. By the time I was fifteen, I was earning more money than my father was, pulling my little cart around and mowing lawns, even for the mayor of the city.

I learned there was a direct association between hard work and a little bit of ingenuity and your income. The earlier that you learn that, that there's a connection between your work and your income, the more likely it is that you're going to be successful in life. Later I went back and worked in factories and mills and construction and so on. And then when I could no longer get a laboring job, I went back into selling.

I used to sell my services door-to-door, selling my lawnmowing services. I sold soap. I sold newspaper subscriptions. I sold Christmas books. I went back into selling, knocking door-to-door. At that time I was paid on straight commission. The joke, we used to say, is that you can only eat what you kill. If you don't make a sale, you don't eat, which is one of the great motivators.

I got it that my income was totally determined on my ability to get results that people would pay me for. In my seminars all over the world I ask this question: "What is your most valuable financial asset?" I let people stew with it for a while, because when I first heard this question I didn't know the answer. Then I realized that your most valuable financial asset is your earning ability. What is your earning ability? It's your ability to get results that people will pay you for, and the most important word for success, in life and in business, is *results*.

Now you might say, *results* sounds very cold. But it's also a matter of results with your family. It's getting results in terms of raising happy, healthy, self-confident children. It's getting results in terms of building a good-quality marriage. It's getting results in terms of helping around the house. The people who get results are the most respected and esteemed people in every single part of life.

Your earning ability is an asset, and all assets, like a piece of machinery or equipment or buildings that yield a return, can be appreciating or depreciating. If it's an appreciating asset, it means that you are becoming worth more and more every day.

There was a story in *Fortune* magazine recently about a woman who worked for the magazine for forty-six years. She finally retired in her seventies. She was one of the most esteemed people that worked there. They had big parties to see her off. They asked her why she had been so valuable to a company like *Fortune* magazine for all these years. She said, "Because I resolved never to go to bed at night without being smarter than I was when I woke up that day. Every single day I learned something new that would help me do my job better."

She did interviews with the Fortune 500 CEOs and presidents and the leading financial lights of the world. She could phone Warren Buffett or Bill Gates or anybody else in the financial world, and they'd take her calls because she was so highly esteemed. That's earning ability. You ask the average person, "What have you done today to increase your value, to increase your ability to get results, to increase your ability to add more value to your world?" Most people are shocked by that.

Einstein said that compounding is the greatest power in the universe. Compounding means each time that you do something to add to your skill level, it compounds with other information you have, and sooner or later all these pieces of information start to come together. It's called the *law of integrative intelligence.* All these pieces of intelligence start to integrate and form a pattern or a design or a template whereby you can see an opportunity to create or build wealth that you hadn't seen before.

Sometimes it's one additional piece of information that transforms everything, that brings together all those pieces of information that you've been gathering for a long period of time. Suddenly they all hit, and suddenly you have a new product or service idea that is transformative.

Look at Steve Jobs and Apple; he came up with this idea of the iPod. All of the technology for the iPod had existed and had been sold by other companies, except for access to the music. What he did was to create a new business model. Today there are fifty-five different types of business models. If you have the wrong business model, your company will drift and often go broke. Business models are changing so fast that 80% or more of companies, including Fortune 500 companies, have broken or obsolete business models, partially or totally.

The new business model is bringing together all of these different factors in a new model that suddenly makes everything transform. A perfect example is Google. They came up with this idea of search. They combined hundreds and then thousands of computers together and then offered the idea of search free so that people can search for information. While they were on the site, they could buy a product or service, and Google could track with algorithms the sort of things that they were interested in and could make those ads pop up. Google created one of the most valuable companies in the world with a new business model.

That business model was basically a free business model. They offered the finest services in the world absolutely free, and while you're here, by the way, here's something else that may help you to be more productive.

Your earning ability is the most important thing of all, and your earning ability is either appreciating or depreciating. Basketball coach Pat Riley once said that either you're getting better or you're getting worse. Nobody stays the same. Every new skill that you develop moves you up the ladder of earning ability. Every new skill means that you are worth more money. Each time you learn a new skill, you step up the ladder; your earning ability increases. If you keep climbing the ladder, your earning ability keeps increasing.

You look the highest-paid people in our society today. They are people who keep climbing skill by skill, day by day, week by week, month by month. They never stop learning new skills. They keep becoming more and more valuable. As a result, people eagerly thrust money in their pockets and pay them millions of dollars as signing bonuses to take senior jobs and pay them millions of dollars in severance pay if they leave for any reason. This is why people earn a lot of money.

The question you always have to ask is, "What have I done today to increase my earning ability, to increase the quality and quantity of results that I can get for people who are willing to pay me for that increase?" If you keep intensely focused on results, the difference it makes in your life is quite extraordinary.

Dan

Brian, give us your own definition of what money is. Talk about how moving from paper money to digital money has helped to show us that money is merely a means of exchange of value and not a thing or a possession. Talk about how this changes a person's perspective on money and how willing they are to spend that money. Some say that money is an energy or a reflection of your life force. Do you agree or disagree, and why?

Brian

The great challenge with digital money, credit card money, bank money, and so on, is that people don't actually handle the bills.

They become divorced from realizing how much money they're spending.

I've seen this with my children. They've grown up in a good home. Then they go off on their own and they buy stuff, and they're quite shocked when the bill comes in. Their friends were all the same. They end up with very large credit card bills and then they get notices, because people want their money. Then the interest starts to rack up, and they're absolutely shocked. It takes them two or three years into their twenties before they go "Whoa!" and they pull back. They destroy their credit cards. They put limits on their credit cards. They pay off the credit cards every month, and they get back on top of it again.

Of course, there's a vested interest on the part of the credit card companies to get you to buy things on credit. There's a vested interest in encouraging people not to think of how much they're spending. It's amazing how many people go bankrupt, personally bankrupt, every year as a result of credit card debt. The major reason for divorce in America, especially among young people in their twenties and thirties, is problems over money. One or the other is spending money. They say, "Well, it's just a credit card." They order stuff online, which is another terrible thing, because then you're doubly divorced from the reality. You click the button, place your order, the stuff comes to your door, and then a couple weeks later the bill appears. "Who bought this? What happened here? Well, I wasn't really thinking. I just did this."

In debt consolidation, when people get deeply in debt, the first thing counselors do is have them tear up their credit cards or consolidate everything into one credit card and put a limit on it so that they can't spend any more in a given month. The credit card is used as a convenience. The next thing is they have the people pay for everything in cash. It's the most phenomenal thing, when you start to pull cash out of your pocket: this is money that you have earned. These are your hourly wages. Suddenly you become crystal clear about how much you're spending, and you stop doing it.

The very act of having to pay cash out of your pocket causes you to become far more thoughtful about expenditures. This is the great challenge people have today.

Money and time are interchangeable in this way: they can be either spent or invested. If you *spend* money or time, it's gone forever, and you can never get it back. If you *invest* it into something that can give you a payoff in the future, then you can benefit from it for the indefinite future. I always say that the best place to invest your time and money is to increase your earning ability. Warren Buffett is the most successful investor in history. He started off with $2000. His companies are worth $350 billion today. His company, Berkshire Hathaway, is third or fourth biggest single company in the United States. Last year he made $25 billion on his companies.

He was asked recently, "Mr. Buffett, you're the greatest investor in history. Where would you say would be the best place to invest today?" He said, without even hesitating, that the best place to invest today is yourself—becoming more valuable at earning the money that you're earning today.

In New York, they did a study and asked 1000 top people this question: if you had $100,000 that you accumulated, where would be the best place to invest it? The consensus was to put it back into becoming better at doing what you did to earn the money in the first place.

If you invest in the stock market or in real estate or anything else, your investment may go up or down. It will be controlled by a hundred factors. It'll be determined by the market and by investment experts and by competition and so on. But if you invest in yourself, you own 100% of the investment forever. You get 100% of the return. You can completely control and direct the investment of your time and money so that you are learning subjects that are most relevant to increasing your most important results right now. If you do these things, then it's the best investment of all.

I say this over and over again: the best investment is to increase your earning ability, to become more and more valuable every single day.

Dan

There's a great misunderstanding about why certain amounts of money are paid to different professions, even when it seems that some of those professions are very important to our society. For example, generally social workers, those who work in elder care, and teachers are paid relatively little compared to investment bankers, lawyers, and lobbyists. Why is it that people in these positions, which are more highly admired by our society, are paid less than those in these less-admired professions?

Brian

One of the great economic laws with regard to labor is supply and demand. If something is in short supply but in great demand, it drives the price up and vice versa. Earl Nightingale summarized this many years ago when he said that you'll always be paid in direct proportion to what you do, how well you do it, and the ease or difficulty of replacing you. If you are a sports star, you can negotiate $100 million contracts because there's no one like you who can make the points and get the network contracts. They'll pay you $100 million because you can hit goals, you can shoot baskets. Look at Michael Jordan, the billion-dollar man.

If you look at these other professions, even though they do helpful jobs in society, the people are easily replaced because there are hundreds of thousands, millions of other people who can do those things. It's a low-skilled job. It does not require a lot of mental effort. It enables people to coast, and the great tragedy about coasting is that you can only do it in one direction.

People take little jobs that require no skill. I saw a woman protesting recently, demanding $15 an hour. She's thirty-four years old. She has seven children. She's earning $8 an hour in fast food, and she's demanding $15-an-hour pay. Well she's thirty-four years old, and she has never raised a finger to increase her skill level so that she'd be worth more money, but she demands that somehow other people pay her money that nobody is willing to pay her because the value of her contribution is so low.

If the value of your contribution is high, another employer will willingly and immediately pay you more money. In fact, the way that employers hire good staff is they find out who's good at the other companies, and they offer them an increase if they'll come and work for them. Eighty-five percent of jobs exchange like that at the highest rate. People pay you more money to come and work for them. The fastest way to get a raise is to do your job so well that your employer will pay you to make sure you don't go somewhere else, where some other employer will pay you more. That's just the way supply and demand works.

I'll give you an example. Citibank received a bailout during the recession. They found that Citibank was paying this one commodities trader $100 million a year in income. They were brought in front of a congressional committee and asked, "How dare you accept money from the government, when you're paying somebody $100 million a year?" They said, "This man works on straight commission, and he generates $4 billion a year in profit for Citibank because he's the most brilliant commodity trader in the world. He has the ability to sense when commodity prices are going to move in a particular direction, and he generates us, the bank, $4 billion a year, and of that we pay him a small commission. We pay him $100 million, which is about 1/400 of the amount that he generates. That's the deal. If we said, we think we're paying you too much, we are surrounded by competitors who would hire him away in an instant and pay him the same or more."

Here's a person who is impossible to replace. This is a person who has spent his entire life learning the skill of commodity trading. Plus he's probably got an enormous special sensitivity, an intuitive sense that nobody has. You put it all together, just like a star athlete. You have to do something that is more highly valued, and you have to do it better than anybody else. You have to develop a reputation.

In my company, I have twenty-two people. I've always given what I call preemptive increases. A preemptive increase means that nobody has to come and say, "Please, can I have some more money? I've been here for an extra year, I've got more experience. Can I have a raise?" No, everybody gets increased pay when their value goes up. They don't have to wait for a year. If it turns out that they're doing great work and they're generating great revenues, then by gum, we offer them more money, not only because they deserve it but because they've earned it. It's just a percentage of the additional value that they're bringing to us. We don't want them to go somewhere else.

Dan

Do you see cash, credit, IOUs, and equity in a home business or an investment as being equal forms of money? Why or why not? What is the difference between each?

Brian

The most important factor is whether or not they yield a return. You invest in your business in order to buy raw materials and hire staff in order to produce products that you can sell at a profit. The loop goes around, which is how all business financing is done.

If you start a business, nobody will lend you any money, because you don't have any track record. I've seen a university professor say to his business students, "When you start your own business, don't use any of your own money. Use only the bank's money. You want to save your own money for your own lifestyle and expenses. So you go to the bank, and you put together an application. You borrow from the bank."

That person is an absolute idiot. I have run businesses for years, and the bank will not lend you a penny if you're just starting a new business. Banks are not in the business of risking money. Banks are in the business of making safe loans. What you have to do is prove to them that this is a safe loan.

I started my existing business twenty-eight years ago in San Diego. I went to the bank to get a line of credit. They said, "We'd be pleased to give you a line of credit, but it has to be cross collateralized." "What do you mean by cross collateral?" "Well, we want a lien against all of your royalty agreements. We want a lien against your house. We want you to deposit $50,000 in an unmovable account. We want a lien against your car and all your furniture. We want collateral equal to five times the amount we're going to lend you."

I said, "That's outrageous." They said, "Take it or leave it." So we took it. That's what you have to do when you start a business. We borrowed a small amount of money. Fortunately we had good cash flow. We had to go into the line every so often, but over time we developed a credit rating. All of those cross collateralizations one by one fell away, and now the only thing they require is a personal guaranty.

They say, "Don't ever give a personal guaranty if you're starting a business." You must be out of your mind. Nobody will even give you a credit card without a personal guaranty.

If you invest in an investment like real estate or a factory for stocks or bonds that pays you a higher return than the cost of the money, that's a good investment. If you invest in other things where the money is spent or gone or has exorbitantly high interest rates, as credit cards do, that's *not* a good investment. A good investment is something that yields cash greater than the cost of money. A bad investment is something that consumes cash with no return.

If you invest money to earn more money, if you invest money in something that's going to give you a return, if you invest in a computer and by using the computer you can speed up technological transfers and the development of intellectual property, and as a result you can earn money, then the computer is a very good investment. It gives you a return on your investment greatly in excess of the cost and depreciation.

Dan

Explain the difference between these concepts: wealth, financial freedom, and income. How are they all related? Can one have a high income but low wealth? Is everyone who is financially independent also very wealthy?

Brian

It's a great question. The joke is that most high-income people are two months away from homelessness because of Parkinson's law. Parkinson's law says that expenses rise to meet income. No matter how much you earn, you spend the same amount and more. The average American lives on about 110% of their income, and the rest of it is on credit cards, loans, financing of their homes, and so on. They are stretching it. They don't have cash.

The average American, when they retire, has a net worth today of about $41,000, plus Social Security—after forty to forty-five years of living and working in the most affluent economy in the history of man. And why is that? It's because they consider high income to be the equivalent of wealth. There is only one kind of wealth that really matters. I learned this from an immigrant who came over here and became extremely wealthy. He said the only income that matters is money that comes from your money. It's money that is thrown off because of your investments.

He said that income is not wealth. Income is merely supporting your lifestyle. The only thing that is wealth is cash flow from other sources. Just remember that: wealth is cash flow from other sources. The wealthiest people that I know always talk about cash flow from other sources. When they analyze an investment—and they'll often take six months to analyze an investment—the question is, will the cash flow from this investment be substantially in excess of the cost of the investment and the cost of the money? Also, will it be in excess of any other alternative use of the money, any alternative investment?

You'll find that the smartest of all people are very, very careful about investing in order to make sure that the return will be greater than the cost of the investment.

Dan

In your opinion, how high a priority should money be in one's life?

Brian

If you ask entrepreneurs, successful or struggling, what money means to them, it always comes back to one word: freedom. Freedom is the reason for being financially successful. Money means that I am free. I used to joke that that meant when you go to a restaurant, you can order without looking at the right-hand column to see how much it costs.

People love freedom. It is one of the most important, if not *the* most important, of all values. Nobody ever feels that they have too much freedom. Many people think that others have too much freedom and that laws should be made against them. Successful people should be taxed and regulated and punished. But the people who say that feel that they themselves should have all the freedom they want.

Author Barbara De Angelis has this wonderful question: "When will you know that you have enough money, and what will you do then?" Money represents freedom, so we look at how much money you will need to feel completely free. One thing I put people through in my business coaching programs is the determination of their number. What is your number? What is the amount that you need to reach in assets and cash flow, monthly and annually, so that you can stop?

Self-made millionaires spend a good deal of time thinking about the answer to this question: how much will I need in order to be able to support the lifestyle I desire, and what will I do then? Then they focus on that, and they sacrifice a lot in the short term in order to finally accumulate that amount of net worth, yielding that amount of income, so that they are free, their family is free, their children are free.

They're not going to stop working, but that's the crossover point. At that point they can get involved in philanthropy and in other activities and cut back. But for the first part of your life, you must put your whole heart into becoming financially free, and you must do it when you have the highest amount of energy, drive, ambition, and opportunity.

Dan

Who are some of the role models and mentors who taught you the most about money? Give a short description of each and the key lesson that each of them taught you about money.

Brian

I have studied books and articles and interviews by and about thousands of successful people over the years—millionaires, billionaires, multibillionaires, going back into history, some of the wealthiest people in history. There were many who started with nothing.

The wealthiest man in history was actually a German banker. His name was Jacob Fugger. He was considered to be the richest man of his age, the richest man in Renaissance Europe. He started off with very little, and then he traded. He was a very good trader, very good lender of money, a very good user of money, a very good supporter of trading ventures, and so on. His whole philosophy was frugality, care, caution, precision, sternness, strictness with regard to money. He became the richest man in Europe.

The Rothschilds started off as a small family and became the richest banking family in Europe and then one of the richest families in the Americas. I've studied these people for years and years and years.

Sometimes you can read an entire book, say on the Rockefellers, and get one idea, one critical idea. John D. Rockefeller became the richest man in the world. One of his ideas was frugality—frugality, saving, and lowering the price of his commodity, which was oil and gas, to the consumer. They called him a robber baron. Yes, he was a robber baron. He put his competitors out of business. He virtually controlled the entire North American oil and gas market.

They brought in the trust busters, and they broke up his company. But what was his great sin? His great sin was that he continually used economies of scale to lower the cost of gas and oil to fuel cars and lights and everything else, so that nobody could offer the product cheaper than he could. Everything he did was to benefit customers, and his competitors considered this to be a terrible thing. So his enemies got together and paid off the government to make laws to break his company up.

They broke up Rockefeller's company into five major oil companies, called "the five sisters." Those companies became the five biggest oil companies in the world, and their competitors still couldn't compete with them, because they kept lowering prices.

These are little things that you pick up. If you want to be successful in business, you have to satisfy your customers with what they want, faster and easier and at lower prices, than anybody else, and you have to continue doing that. That's one of the great financial lessons of all, which we'll talk about in depth later.

Dan

Brian, what is the biggest misconception that most people have about money, and how can they correct it?

Brian

Harvard University concluded that the number one quality of financially successful people is *longtime perspective*. Today we have an economy where people are impatient for immediate gratification. It's just killing people's hopes and dreams. Longtime perspective means that you make decisions in the short term that will have great rewards in the long term, which means that you work hard and you save your money and you invest it carefully.

You let it accumulate with the miracle of compounding, which we'll come back to.

Today, 65% of American adults think that the only way they will be able to retire financially independent is if they win the lottery. Most people think that financial success is a crap game, and so they see a Mark Zuckerberg, who becomes a billionaire in his twenties. They don't understand that he is one of millions of people who've tried to do this. But for Zuckerberg everything came together, the stars all aligned—the advent of the Internet, the advent of rapid data processing, the opening of social media. Everything came together for him at that one point in time.

Other people have made hundreds of millions and billions as well, but they are extraordinarily rare. Most people make their money by working hard, contributing value, saving their money, investing it carefully, and letting it accumulate over time.

TWO

The Myths About Money

Before we begin explaining the laws of money, we need to clear the deck of the numerous misconceptions, half-truths, and outright lies about the subject. If any of these ideas lurk in the recesses of your mind, they can tempt you to take an invalid road to wealth, which ultimately leads to a dead end. Brian calls these false ideas *the myths about money*. He'll describe the foundational idea behind each of the myths and then clearly identify each myth in detail.

Dan

Brian, let's begin this chapter by discussing the foundational idea that underlies most of the myths of money: the idea of getting something for nothing. Discuss how this idea is a violation of the scientific law of cause and effect, and how it can lead one to waste years on false roads to wealth that lead only to broken dreams and an empty bank account.

Brian

There are many reasons why people stay poor all of their lives. The *law of belief* says that whatever you believe with feeling becomes your reality. Many people believe things that are completely impossible with regard to money. In *Alice in Wonderland*, Alice says to the Mad Hatter, "You can't possibly believe that. It's impossible." And the Mad Hatter says, "No, I've developed the ability to believe at least two impossible things before breakfast every day."

An enormous number of people believe things that simply aren't true. The humorist Josh Billings used to say, "It ain't what a man knows what hurts him, it's what he knows that ain't true." This is fatal to financial success.

I'd like to start off by talking about the greatest of all laws, which really determines everything that happens to you. Three hundred and fifty years before Christ, Aristotle, the great philosopher, formulated the Aristotelian principle of causality, what we today call the *law of cause and effect*. At a time when everyone believed in gods and miracles and fortune and so on, he said, no, no, we live in an orderly universe, where everything happens for a reason; for every effect, there is a cause or specific causes. If you wish to achieve an effect, you must be very clear about what the effect is, and then trace it back to the causes.

So if you want to double your income, find somebody who is earning twice as much as you in your own field. Then trace it back to what they did to get there. You find that everybody who's earning twice as much as you today was at one time earning half as much. So they must have done specific things.

If you ask them, they'll tell you. If you don't know them personally, read their books and their articles and their interviews, and they will tell you, because people who earn a lot of money are very generous in telling other people how they did it. If you do what other successful people have done over and over again, you get the same result, based on the law of cause and effect.

We live in a world governed by law, not by chance. It's not luck. It's not coincidence. The law of cause and effect says that everything happens for a reason. There's a cause for every effect. This is the iron law of human destiny. It says that everything happens for a reason, whether we know what it is or not. It's a law, and that means that you can control your future.

Every effect, success or failure, wealth or poverty, has a specific cause or causes. Every cause or action has an effect or consequence of some kind or another, whether we can see it or not or whether we like it or not. Sir Isaac Newton, who is considered the greatest physicist in history, called this the *law of action and reaction*. He said for every action there is an equal and opposite reaction, and this is a law of the universe.

In other words, if you put in value, you get value back—action and reaction. If you don't put in value, you don't get value back. You cannot violate the laws of nature. Napoleon Hill, author of *Think and Grow Rich*, said, never try to violate the laws of nature and expect to win. It's a major reason for success.

This law of cause and effect says that all achievement, all wealth, all happiness, all prosperity, and all success are the direct and indirect effects, or results, of specific causes or actions. Earl Nightingale used to say that a person would not sit in front of the empty stove and say, "Give me some heat, and then I'll put in some wood." That's not the way it works. First you put in the wood, and then you get the heat. First you put in, and then you take out.

It would be like the farmer saying to the field, "Give me a crop, and then I'll plant some seed." The world is full of people who say, "If they want me to work harder, they should pay me more." No, what you do is you work harder and produce more, then they will pay you more—inevitably—or someone else will.

This law means that if you can be clear about the effect or result that you want, you can probably achieve it. You can study others who've accomplished the same goal, and by doing what they did, you can get the same results. I teach business courses all over the world. I teach what I call the Two-Day MBA, and then the Two-Day DBA or Doctor of Business Administration, and now I teach a course called Business Model Reinvention. These are all based on established, proven principles that people have discovered in building successful businesses. I go around the world like Johnny Appleseed, who planted apple seeds and grew apple orchards in his trail. People come back to me a year later and say they've transformed their business. They stopped doing this. They started doing that. They'd never heard of these things before, and their businesses are transformed.

Sometimes people change their business 500%. I was in Helsinki recently. A man had been in my seminar the year before. He said he went back and changed their entire business model, and they've increased their business fifty times in twelve months. They've gone from being a struggling startup to being one of the most successful businesses in the country. It's phenomenal what they've accomplished.

He was using the law of cause and effect. There are certain causes that bring about this effect. They weren't doing these things before, and they were puzzled why they weren't getting the effects of increased sales and profitability.

When you identify these causes and implement them in your own life and activities, you'll get the same results that hundreds of thousands and even millions of others have gotten. An interesting point, by the way: In the year 1900, there were 5000 millionaires in the world. When I started studying this subject in 1980, there were 1 million, most of them in America. By the year 2000, there were 7 million. Today there are 10 million, and the number is growing by about 10–12% per year. So millions and millions of people have started from nothing to become millionaires by doing certain things in a certain way.

If only one person had become a millionaire, than you could say that was a rare accident. With two, you could say it's a coincidence. But if millions and millions of people from every single background with every limitation that you could imagine become millionaires, then there are obviously some laws and principles at work.

If you can study others who have achieved the same goal, you can get the same results. You can acquire whatever amount of money you really want if you will just do what others have done before to achieve the same results, and if you don't, you won't. It's as simple as that.

One thing I have learned is that nature is blind. Nature doesn't care. It's not as if there is some great power in the universe that wants you to be a big success. Nature is quite neutral. Nature just simply says, like justice with her eyes closed, that if you do what other successful people do, you get the same results, and if you don't you don't.

I was quite offended when I first heard that. But it's the greatest guarantor of success that there is. You can be a complete jerk, you can be tall or short, or black or white, or educated or uneducated, or a new immigrant or here for generations, it doesn't matter. That's why everybody wants to go to America, Australia, New Zealand, England, and Finland, countries where they have an entrepreneurial ethic, because you can start with nothing and become financially successful. Every time I go to these countries, I meet people that come from India, from China, people from all over the world, who are millionaires, who went there and just began to do what other successful entrepreneurs do.

The most important expression of this universal law of cause and effect is that thoughts are causes and conditions are effects. To put it another way, thought is creative. Your thoughts are the primary creative forces in your life. You create your entire world by the way you think. All the people and situations of your life have been created by your own thinking. When you change your thinking, you change your life, sometimes in seconds.

The most important principle of personal or business success is simply this; you become what you think about most of the time. This was Earl Nightingale's strangest secret, but it was also repeated back in the Bible: "As a man thinketh in his heart, so is he." It'll be unto you according to your thoughts or your faith. Even Emerson said this in 1858: a person becomes what they think about all day long.

The great principle is that your outer world is a reflection of your inner world. So it's not what happens to you, but how you *think about* what happens to you that determines how you feel and react. It's not the world outside of you that dictates your circumstances or conditions. It's the world inside of you that creates the conditions of your life.

Specifically, it's the way you think about money and your financial situation that largely determines your financial conditions today. People who come from homes that are well off are much more likely to become financially successful in life, because that's what they've grown up with. That's what they've seen around them. That's what they've heard about, and so their worldview is that if you work hard and offer value, then you can be financially successful as well.

Here's an important point with regard to this principle, and it has to do with one of the major reasons why people fail. It is one of the worst of all vices—the vice of envy. Envy and resentment are like twin sisters. They go around together arm in arm. If you envy other people, you resent them. If you resent them, you want to hurt them or bring them down.

There is an entire political philosophy that is aimed at people who envy and resent the more successful. But here's what happens: if you envy and resent successful people, you automatically set up a negative force field within yourself. This drives out any chance for you to ever be successful or happy, unless you do it dishonestly, or you win the lottery.

If you envy and resent other people, if you criticize them and pull them down, if you engage in snide, gossipy negative conversations about them, it has no effect on the other person. They don't even know that you're doing it, and frankly they don't care, but it destroys all your hopes and dreams for success. Never allow yourself to be in a conversation where people are running down or criticizing successful people. They say, "Oh, yeah, they may be rich, but they're not happy."

The rich have been studied at great length, and I can tell you this: they are very happy. They are very happy that their problems are small compared to their opportunities. Therefore, always praise successful people and look up to them with admiration.

Learn from them. Speak well about them. Be happy for their success. Then you start to create a force field of energy that draws to you opportunities to be like them as well.

People say that your income will be the average income of the five people you associate with most of the time, Whether or not that's true, it's a very good way to think. Your average net worth will be the average net worth of the people you associate with. Why? It's because you develop the same thinking styles and attitudes as these people.

Napoleon Hill said the greatest principle of success that he learned was the Mastermind principle. In the Mastermind, you get together on a regular basis with other success-oriented people, and you talk over what you've learned, and what you've read, and what's working for you, and what you've discovered, and so on.

This Mastermind cross-fertilizes all the minds, so everybody at the Mastermind is thinking positively about each other and about their own possibilities. The Mastermind seems to be a triggering factor for all great wealth. You start to associate with other people who are at your same level or higher, and you start to become like them. I can tell you stories of Masterminds that are absolutely phenomenal.

Whatever you truly believe with feeling becomes your reality. The greatest challenge that we have is self-limiting beliefs. We believe that we are limited in some way or in many ways. For me, what held me back for several years was I was told that if you don't get a good education, if you don't graduate from high school and go to college, you'll never be successful. I bombed out of high school. I didn't pass.

I worked at laboring jobs for several years, and I just accepted that I was a laborer. If I lost a laboring job, I went and looked for another laboring job. If I lost a job washing dishes, I got a job washing cars. If I lost my job washing cars, I got a job in construction or janitorial services, or stacking wood in a lumberyard, or putting nuts on bolts in a factory. I just looked for laboring jobs, because I was told that if you don't get a good education, you won't do well in life.

I accepted that until I got into sales, at the very bottom, and finally started to become successful. I started to make a lot of money, more money, even, than people around me who had degrees from the best universities. Suddenly I realized I'd been sold a bill of goods.

The starting point of success, which I began teaching in my seminars more than thirty years ago, is to question your self-limiting beliefs. There's a story about the devil. The devil is showing a person around hell like a tourist. He shows him all the ways he uses to get people into hell. He shows greed and dishonesty and alcoholism and dope addiction and criminality. These are all the ways that he destroys people on earth to get them into hell when they die.

The devil takes this man into a special room, and the room is completely darkened. In the middle of the room there's a showcase, like a jeweler's showcase. There's one pinpoint of light, and it shines down on the item inside this glass-enclosed showcase. It looks like a wedge that you would put under a door to hold it open. And the devil says, "This is my favorite of all. This brings more people into hell than any other factor in human life." And the visitor says, "Well, what is it? It looks like a door wedge." The devil says, "No, no, no. This is the wedge of self-doubt. Once I can get this into a person's mind, where they start to doubt themselves and their abilities, to doubt their abilities to be successful or to practice self-discipline, or to work hard or save their money—if I can get them to doubt themselves, then all their strength disappears. Sooner or later they come and join me here in hell for eternity."

Self-doubt is a limiting belief, and you have to realize that if you can overcome those limiting beliefs, you can change your life. Here's what I teach people. I say, "Imagine that there is a belief store. You can go to this belief store and you can buy a belief and put it into your subconscious master program. If you could buy any belief at all, what would be the best one to buy?" The answer is to buy the belief that you are going to be a big success in life. Plug that in, and just keep repeating to yourself, "No matter what happens. I am going to be a big success in life."

Look for every trace of evidence to prove this. Someone gives you a compliment because you did something well. You say, "It's true; I'm on the road to becoming a big success in life." When you read a book and you find a new idea on how to be more successful and set goals, say, "Yes, this is part of my plan. I'm going to be a big success in life."

W. Clement Stone died worth $800 million, which would be several billion dollars today. He started with nothing, selling papers on the streets of Chicago, with no father, his mother taking care of him. He taught everybody this principle of becoming an inverse paranoid. Now a paranoid is someone who believes that everything is part of a conspiracy to hurt them and to drag them down. Many people are paranoids. They are catastrophists. No matter what happens, they think of the worst outcome that can possibly happen from it. It's very common in certain upbringings.

Stone said, instead, whenever something goes wrong, imagine that there is a massive conspiracy out there, not to hurt you but to make you successful. So with everything that happens to you, look into it and say, "That's good. I wonder what there is about this that I can use to become more successful. Because I'm going to be a big success in life."

I learned this many years ago, before I began speaking. When my children were born, one after another, as soon as they could understand a little bit of English, I began telling them, "By the way, you're going to be a big success in life." As they grew old, I would tell them, "You're going to be a big success in life."

As each one of them came into the world and grew up, I would tell them, "You're going to be a big success in life." And they would say, "Yes, but what, and how, and I don't know, and what will I do?" I said, "Don't worry, you'll try lots of things, but you are going to be a big success in life."

I would repeat this over and over, because I know that the influence of parental figures is enormous when children are young. You can actually send them messages that bypass their conscious minds and become permanently logged into their subconscious and just proceed on automatic. So I knew what I was doing. I would repeat this over and over and over again. And now my children have grown up, and all of them are absolutely convinced that they're going to be big successes in life. They work hard. They're honest. They're popular. They're friendly. They're positive. They're never negative. They're never depressed. They're just happy and thoroughly engaged in their work and their activities, and they're doing well, because I programmed them at a young age with the message that no matter what happens, you are going to be a big success in life. That overrides and cancels out every temporary failure or difficulty that they have.

So if one of your goals is to be financially successful, one of the scientific principles is to absolutely believe that you are going to be a big financial success. Look at everything that happens to you as part of a great conspiracy that's organized by the universe to make you successful. Then you'll start to say, "Wow, I had this setback, I learned this lesson."

Many young people start a business adventure and go broke, or it fails completely, and they lose all their time and money. This happens over and over again. And in retrospect they say, "Thank heavens I went broke and lost all my money, because if that hadn't happened, I might still be struggling with that company. Years may have passed, with no success. Now I'm wealthy because of that terrible thing that happened in the past."

That's the key to overcoming this myth that you have any limits at all. The fact is that nobody's better than you and nobody is smarter than you. Anything that other people have done, within reason, you can do as well. You never compare yourself with billionaires or multibillionaires. You compare yourself with other people you went to school with who are doing better than you.

Again, this comes out in the most recent research: successful people always compare themselves one up. It's called *social comparison theory*. It's been validated by research at Harvard by Leon Festinger. People compare themselves with upwardly mobile, successful people. No matter what they accomplish, they look at the next step up on the ladder.

The idea is to be like the people who are higher on the ladder, and not to tear them down. Trying to tear them down, even mentally or verbally, has no effect on them, but it destroys your chances for financial success, so be careful what you say and think, because you do become what you think about most of the time.

Dan

Let's discuss each of the myths in detail. Myth number one: you can attract money and wealth into your life using the power of your mind—the essential idea behind the law of attraction. Describe this idea in popular culture and why it is at best a half-truth.

Brian

This law goes back 4000 years. The people who have written about the law of attraction often have only a superficial understanding of it. I began studying the metaphysical work of the ancient masters many, many years ago, and got into it in great depth.

The law of attraction says that you are a living magnet and that you invariably attract into your life the people, situations, and circumstances that are in harmony with your dominant thoughts. So when you think a thought, remember: you become what you think about.

The law of attraction must be considered in combination with other laws, including the *law of correspondence*, which says that your outer world is a reflection of your inner world. Wherever you look, there you are. It's almost like you are living in a 360-degree mirror that surrounds you. Wherever you look, you see yourself, and your thinking, your predominant thinking, is reflected in the conditions of your life in three major areas: your health, your companions, and your financial situation.

First of all, your health reflects the way that you think about food, nutrition, diet, exercise, and so on. A quick aside: they did a study on this. Why is it that some people are thin, and some people are overweight? The answer was that thin people—using the principle of long-term thinking—think of how they are likely to feel and look the next day after eating today, so they are a little bit more discriminating in their diet, because they like to feel light and trim and healthy.

Overweight people think only about the sensation and pleasure at the moment of eating. They're preoccupied with how good it feels. And since your appestat, which is your desire to eat food, only lasts for about twenty or thirty minutes after the first bite, they eat as fast as they can and as much as they can until their appestats shut off. As a result, they expand the size of their stomachs, which means that they can eat more and more.

People who are overweight are gorgers. People who are underweight are thinking that tomorrow they want to look and feel trim. So you can always tell what a person thinks about most of the time.

The second area has to do with your relationships: you always attract into your life the kind of people that are in harmony with your dominant thoughts. So a really positive person seems to be surrounded by other really positive people.

The final area has to do with your financial condition. You can tell what a person thinks about money most of the time by what they're attracting into their lives.

That's the starting point, but it has so much more depth than this. Some people have written books that say, all you have to do is think happy thoughts and visualize wealth and success and you'll attract it, but that's simply not true. In the Bible it says faith without works is dead. And there's a little ditty that says, pray but move your feet. What it says is that you have to work very, very hard to set up that force field of energy. It's not possible to set up a permanent force field of energy for financial success if you are not constantly doing things that are consistent and in harmony with it.

Another principle is called the *law of vibration*. This law is known throughout the musical world. It's also known that every single substance in the world is in vibration, like a tuning fork. Rocks and stones vibrate; certain plants and animals give off vibrations. Here's an example: imagine a large room with a piano on either side of the room, and you go to one piano and you hit the note of C flat. You walk across the room to the other piano, and the note of C flat will be vibrating in sympathetic harmony with the first one.

This vibration, or what we call sympathetic resonance, is what you see in relationships. The poet Kahlil Gibran wrote about this 100 years ago. He said that when you meet your husband or wife, there will be a moment of meeting, a sympathetic resonance. At this moment, when the eyes meet, this resonance will take place immediately, within seconds. It will take place at that moment, or it will never happen.

For people who have been happily married for any period of time, a question that they're asked is, how did you meet? Both will remember that instant of sympathetic vibration across a crowded room. Their eyes met, and there was a harmony or a vibration that brought them together. They say when you meet your soul mate, you recognize that you've just met your best friend. And that's it, there's no drama. There's no trauma. There are no violent ups and downs. It's just there. You just walk away together, and you're together ever after. My wife and I have been married for thirty-six years, and we met in just one moment. We still recall to the instant the second our eyes met. This is part of the law of attraction.

The flip side of the law of attraction, which they don't talk about, is called the *law of repulsion*. If you take two magnets and you try to push the same poles together; the magnets will push apart. This is a part of many electrical devices. The motor will spin in a certain way, but if the magnets are put in wrong, it won't work at all. Therefore, if you think a negative thought, then what will happen is you will actually repel out of your life what it is you want to have. That's why I said you never think negative thoughts about people who are financially successful. You actually repel all hopes that you could ever have to be financially successful.

Some have negative ideas with regard to money, like "Rich people are bad." It's usually taught to you by your parents when you're young. Usually they're poor and they're angry and so on. "Rich people are bad." If you believe that, then you'll never be financially successful, because you'll be sabotaging yourself.

That's why so many people engage in self-sabotage after they make a lot of money. Comic Robin Williams had this funny one-liner. He said that cocaine is God's way of telling you you're making too much money. Every so often you have cases where a taxi driver will report that somebody left a briefcase full of money in their cab, or people will lose a large amount of money some other way. It will fall out of their car on the street. These are all subconscious acts of self-sabotage, where a person does not believe they deserve their success.

Another important part of the law of attraction is feeling deserving. It is such a big issue that almost all problems come from people believing that they do not deserve to have good things happen to them. They work extremely hard on the outside, but inside they have a negative vibration. On the outside, they actually work themselves to death. They'll work sixteen hours a day. Sometimes they'll overdrink, they'll overeat. They'll destroy their marriages and their families. They'll have heart disease and other illnesses and so on. They'll make a lot of money, and then they'll sabotage themselves, because deep down inside they don't believe they deserve it. They've set up this law of repulsion, which takes all the success that they have so desperately worked to achieve, and it drives the success out of their lives.

I had a friend who built one of the biggest and most successful businesses in the United States—a multimillion-dollar business. He came from a very poor background. One day his accountant came to him and said, "You know, if we were to do a couple of little mechanical changes on the cash registers, we could carve off a few cents per transaction, and it would kind of disappear into a separate account."

At the beginning, he needed the money. But as the business grew and grew, this amount became millions of dollars, and he got caught, because the same person who had introduced him to the idea was given a chance to roll or go to prison. So he rolled on his boss, whom he'd sold into the idea. His boss—wealthy, successful beyond imagination, a national legend—was sent to prison for eight years. Just the most incredible thing. Because of his poor background, he had this feeling that somehow he didn't deserve it, so he engaged in acts of self-sabotage.

The law of attraction is your thoughts emotionalized. It's like a lamp. You could have a lamp, and you could say that this lamp should give off a wonderful light, but not if it's not plugged in to electricity. A thought by itself has no emotional context. It's neutral. It's basically an inert substance. It's only when you multiply the thought times an emotion that the thought starts to have power.

This is why we say that everything you have in your life is attracted to you by the way you think. You can change your life, because you can change the way you think. When you develop a burning desire for financial success and think about it all the time, you set up a force field of positive emotional energy that attracts people, ideas, and opportunities into your life to help you make your goals into realities.

There's a fingerlike part of your brain called the reticular cortex, which is responsible for the reticular activating system. When you emotionalize a thought or a desire, you actually send a message to that part of your brain, which then becomes hypersensitive to anything in your external world that may enable you to bring about that desire.

Say you decide you want to own a red sports car: you suddenly start to see red sports cars everywhere. You see ads for red sports cars. You see red sports cars turning corners two and three blocks away. You see red sports cars parked in garages and driveways. It's because you've told your subconscious mind that you are interested in a red sports car. This is part of the law of attraction.

If you decide you want to take a vacation to Hawaii, you start to see advertisements for vacations. If you decide you want to lose weight, you see advertisements for weight loss everywhere. This is the way your brain helps you to succeed in life. It helps you to survive and thrive.

Look at your financial life today, and see how it harmonizes with your thinking. Take full credit for all the good things in your life. They are there because you have attracted them to yourself. And look around at the things you don't like, and take full responsibility for them as well. They are there because of you as well, because of some flaw in your own thinking.

What is that flaw, and what are you going to do about it? What is it that you're attracting into your life, or what is it that you are not attracting? Let's take a very simple example: self-made millionaires. I started researching this many years ago. I was asked by a company if I would give their 800 independent business owners, distributors, a lecture on how to become self-made millionaires. I said, of course.

I hung up the phone and I realized that I was thirty-eight years old. I always wanted to be a self-made millionaire from the time I was a teenager, like everybody else, but I was still broke and still struggling and still in debt. And I didn't really know much about self-made millionaires.

I had two months before I gave this talk. So I sat down and did some research. I began to do some reading. I started off with *The Millionaire Next Door* and *Selling to the Affluent*, both by Thomas Stanley. I started to realize that self-made millionaires are people who have a mind-set that attracts wealth. This mind-set is a series of ways in which they think most of the time. If you think the way they think most of the time, you start to set up a very, very high level of vibration. This vibration emanates from you like radio waves and, like a magnet, starts to draw into your life all the things that you need.

Then I went and gave this talk. It was very well received. It was called "The Twenty-One Success Secrets of Self-Made Millionaires." I was asked to give it again. And again. I originally gave it in a one-hour form, and then someone said, "Well, we have a ninety-minute slot. Can you give it ninety minutes?" "Yes." "How about half a day?" Eventually I gave it over a full-day period. It took an entire day, six to seven hours of delivery with breaks and lunch, to deliver this seminar, because I kept expanding on each of the twenty-one principles.

The most interesting thing happened—within five years, I was a millionaire. The more I taught these principles, the more

I thought about these principles, and the more I practiced them. You become what you think about most of the time. You also become what you teach most of the time. So if you start to teach these principles to someone else, you start to internalize them at a deeper level. You start to increase the intensity of vibration. If you teach these principles with conviction, and you really feel strongly about them, and you try to get people enthusiastic about them, you start to resonate at a higher level. More and more things start to happen that attract money, and more and more money comes into your life.

Most self-made millionaires come from business, but most of them became millionaires without even realizing it. One year, after several years of work, their accountants told them, "By the way, you're worth more than $1 million now." They said, "Really? How did that happen?" They were so busy doing their work, so focused on their work and getting paid really well for it, that they weren't even looking at the accumulation of wealth; it just happened.

That's what happened to me. I sat down because I had to fill out a form to borrow money from the bank, and you had to list all of your assets. I had to collect them all and write them out clearly. I thought, "Oh my God, I'm worth $1.1 million this year." I had to call my wife. This is real net worth. This is what banks consider to be value—home equity, assets in the company, savings accounts, stocks and bonds, and so forth.

The more you study the field, the more you set up this field of vibration. The more you think clearly, the more you will attract what you think about into your life. For example, if you want to become a millionaire, imagine a check made out to your name for $1 million. Just think of the check. Just look at the check. Just imagine that check made payable to you for $1 million and put a date on it.

There is a famous story about Jim Carrey, the actor, who wrote out a check to himself for $10 million for one movie. This was when he was a junior comedian. He had moved down from Toronto to Hollywood, and he would go and sit up in the Hollywood hills and look at his check. The check was made out to Jim Carrey: $10 million for one movie. He would look at this check over and over again, and within a few years he was offered $10 million to star in a movie. He said it was exactly the amount that he had written on the check.

Read and feed this picture. You see, every time you feed a picture of your desired goal into your mind, your subconscious mind takes it like a snapshot, puts it into your permanent subconscious programming, and sees it over and over again.

Another way that you can see it is to see yourself doing the work that you would be doing to earn the money. Many salespeople will visualize themselves selling big products, selling big accounts, closing big deals, whether it's in insurance, or ships, or planes, or stocks, or bonds. They'll see themselves mentally, visualize themselves interacting with customers, seeing the customers smiling and signing the check and signing the contract.

Another way you can do it—and this is what my wife and I did—is to start looking at the kind of home that you will live in when you're wealthy. Every Saturday my wife Barbara and I would go to open houses in the wealthiest neighborhoods. We'd walk through really expensive homes, talking about what we'd like to see in our house. We'd talk about having this and that, having a staircase and a backyard, a pool, a gym, and all of those things. Within about three years after doing this, we had moved from a rented house to a beautiful house in a beautiful neighborhood, which we sold. Then we moved from Canada to California, and looked at 150 houses and walked into this house.

We both looked at each other, and we knew this was the house. This was the house we had visualized, written down, talked about, and the price, terms, everything we could afford, they accepted. Everything just fit together neatly, and we've been in that house for twenty-eight years. As you get older and your kids move away, you think of moving to something smaller, but we don't ever want to move away from this house. They probably will have to carry us out, as they say.

In other words, it was exactly the house that we'd envisioned. We had written down forty-two things we wanted in a perfect house. After we'd seen this house, we checked off the checklist. It had all forty-two, the most amazing thing.

That's how you set up the force field. You pray. In other words, you pray, visualize, get a clear mental picture of what you want, and then move your feet. Because it's only in moving your feet that you actually hit the tuning fork. This is when you hit the tuning fork and set up the vibration. If you don't do anything, faith without actions is dead. If you don't do anything, nothing happens.

Unfortunately, in all the stuff that's written about the law of attraction, the word *work* never appears. They imagine that you can have something for nothing, and—going back to what we talked about before—this is one of the worst myths of all, this something-for-nothing myth. It says I can take out more than I put in.

The fact is you can only take out a small part of the value that you create. You get a slice of the big, as they say in New York. You get a percentage of commission on the value that you create. So you can only take out what you put in, and if you don't put in, you can't take out.

This idea of something for nothing is killing so many people in so many fields all over the world. This misconception, this myth that you can get something out without putting something in, is turning people into mental criminals. They're angry at those who have earned money. They demand that their money be turned over to them by the force of government, that money be taken away from the successful, that the successful be punished and so on, and that they should be given money that they do not deserve and that they have not earned. That's the problem with the idea of something for nothing. As you know, I've written and recorded extensively on the subject. Practically every single aspect of the problems in the world today is an example of expecting something for nothing.

Einstein spent his whole life looking for a unified field theory. This theory would be the one physical principle that would explain everything on earth. Einstein was interested in physics, not humans. I spent almost thirty years looking for a unified field theory of human life. I found it. I call it the *E factor*. This stands for the *expediency factor*, and it says that human beings are neither good nor bad, but they always seek the fastest and easiest way to get the things they want with little or no concern for secondary consequences.

If you understand that, it explains all the problems. It explains criminality. It explains welfare. It explains unemployment. It explains drunkenness, lack of application, laziness. It explains all your social problems, all your international problems, dictators, thieves, criminals, marauders. All of the wars have been wars of plunder throughout history.

The first thing the Nazis did in World War II was to plunder the countries they invaded. They plundered them and stole everything that wasn't nailed down and most things that *were* nailed down. They were simply wars of plunder. They stole and stole and stole.

Look at every single conqueror. Saddam Hussein had, what, nineteen palaces? While his people were eating dirt, he built billion-dollar palaces. The recent head of the Ukraine had billion-dollar palaces. Putin is now worth many billions of dollars. It's just pure plunder, something for nothing. It's very easy to slip into it, because it's very easy to rationalize.

So the desire to get something for nothing, the desire, to get something that you have not earned and do not deserve, is one of the things that destroys all the hopes and dreams of people worldwide.

Dan

Brian, I know you are a fan of Ayn Rand. She had a quote that goes as follows: "Moochers look to acquire money, usually other people's money." Using this quote as a backdrop, let's discuss myth number two: wealthy people spend their time thinking of ways to acquire money. Discuss why this is untrue, because the vast majority of wealthy people today spend time looking for ways to create value and/or wealth; money is actually the by-product, not the focal point. The productive citizen looks to add value through productive work, a new invention, or a new business, which generates equity in the form of a salary, an appreciating asset, etc. How does this comply with the law of cause and effect?

Brian

The idea that wealthy people think about getting money all the time is incorrect. The most important principle in human life is the principle of *service*. Earl Nightingale said that your rewards will always be equal to the value of your service to others. The question that you need to ask every day is, what can I do to increase the value of my service to others today?

Go back to the teachings of Jesus and the teachings of most of the great prophets. They have to do with serving others, serving the less fortunate. The wonderful thing is that human beings are uniquely designed, in our DNA, so that our greatest joy comes from serving other people.

I was having dinner with my son and his wife, and they have two little girls. My son's a great father, and she's a great mother. The little girls are just as happy as can be. All the parents think about is doing things for their little girls. Having children and taking care of your children is one of the greatest joys that a person can have. People say, "Oh, they're terrible at this age, they're terrible at that age." They're never terrible. Having kids and taking care of our kids gives us so much pleasure that we'll spend our whole lives for them. We'll even put up with a lack of appreciation from them when they grow up.

The average man will die eight years younger than the average woman, because he'll work himself to death to provide for his family. Serving his family gives him joy, to the point of being willing to work himself senseless.

Service is critical. Of course wealthy people, successful people, want to earn a lot of money, but money is a way of measuring whether or not you're actually serving people. Money is a way of measuring whether or not what you're doing works, whether it's profitable. Money is the market's way, nature's way, of telling you that this is a valuable expenditure of time and effort. Many people don't understand this. So serving is what people look for. Whenever I'm traveling, I look for products and services that can really help people.

Let's go back to John D. Rockefeller. John D. Rockefeller was a piker. He started off earning $3.75 a week as a clerk at the very bottom of a company. He gave $1.75 a week to charity. That's how he started his life: he gave half of his earnings to charity, and then he saved a little bit and accumulated. He was always looking for ways to serve others. People used kerosene lanterns. He was one of the first people to find ways to produce kerosene.

Then, when the combustion engine and the automobile came along, his whole focus was on serving people by giving them the products that they needed to enhance their lives at lower prices. He owned everything from the oil fields to the pumps to the pipelines to the railroads to the refineries, all the way through to the gas station, so that he could keep lowering the price without paying the middleman, so he could serve more and more people at lower and lower prices.

Look at Henry Ford. Henry Ford revolutionized the world of manufacturing. When people were doing team manufacturing, it took about 300 hours to make a car, because a team would do everything. In conjunction with his engineers, Ford developed the production line, where they could manufacture cars at such speed that a car could sell for $300 rather than $3000.

The people actually building the cars, working men, who were basically the lowest level of society at that time, could afford to buy the product they were making. Henry Ford transformed the entire world, and this was his greatest joy. He became very close to the richest man in the world at the peak of his powers by making cars available to everybody, which no one had ever done before.

Cars had been for the wealthy. Cars were for people who could spend two or three year's worth of the average working man's earnings. But now the average person could buy a car. And then somebody came up with the idea of a down payment and payment terms. So the workingman could buy a car with a small down payment and pay it off over three years. It transformed everything.

Let's look at Sears Roebuck, which became one of the biggest retailers in the history of the world because they came up with the money-back guarantee, no questions asked. Nobody had ever done that in history. They said you couldn't do that. Sears said, "The people we serve are good people, and if we sell them a product through our catalog, the only reason they'll send it back is because it wasn't what they thought they ordered, it was the wrong size, the wrong color, or something else. We're going to offer an unconditional guarantee." It turned out that less than 5% of people ever asked for their money back. What they asked for was an exchange; 99.9% said, "Can I just change it for a different color or a different size?" Sears Roebuck went on to become one of the most profitable retailers in history.

Look at Walmart today. I really love Walmart. I worked for them a couple of years ago, and I was addressing one of their conventions. I did a whole one-day seminar for one of their divisions. In the midst of their annual convention in St. Louis—they had 25,000 people there; I was speaking to 2000 managers—the president of Walmart came in, and everybody stopped.

He came in, and he gave a speech. It was about five minutes long. He said that we at Walmart have a very simple philosophy:

we represent people who live from paycheck to paycheck, who have no extra money and who cannot afford to make a buying mistake. Our job is to get them the very best selection of products at the lowest possible prices by using our buying power, and then to unconditionally guarantee everything we sell so that nobody ever gets stuck with a product or gets stuck paying more for a product anywhere else. Our job is to help our clients improve the quality and standard of their lives so that they can buy more of the things that they want and need for their family.

He gave that talk, and he gave it with such passion! Everybody in that room jumped to their feet cheering, because that's the Walmart philosophy: serve our customers. Every single thing we do is to get prices down lower and lower so our customers can buy more and more of the things they need to improve the quality of their lives.

Look at Walmart, with 11,000 stores—the most successful retail operation in history. Everybody there is passionate about serving others. By the way, the Walton family is worth about $149 billion today because Sam Walton divided up his entire inheritance before he died. If you were to take just Sam Walton's family, they would be by far, almost by 100%, the richest single family in the world because of this incredible ethic of service.

That's how wealthy people think. When wealthy people look at a hotel or real estate development, or a store, or a stock, or a product, they're always looking at how they can develop a product or service that will help people improve the quality of their lives. That's what they think about all the time. That's what they get excited about, and that's what they get rewarded for.

Dan

Let's discuss myth number three: it's impossible to reach your financial goals, let alone become wealthy, if you are an employee. Does this mean that the vast majority of nonentrepreneurs have no way of becoming wealthy or financially independent? Describe how, through following a disciplined plan of spending and saving, anyone can become financially free, even if it might take longer than for a business owner.

Brian

Peter Lynch was the most successful investor in history. He built the Magellan investment fund, a multibillion dollar fund, and then retired wealthy. He said these wonderful words: "It's not timing the market, it's time *in* the market that counts."

If a person buys shares of stock in a mutual fund or index fund, they're actually becoming owners, because each share of stock represents a percentage of ownership of that company. Ten percent of self-made millionaires are people who worked for another company all of their lives. They worked really hard, were paid well, and they saved their money. They took advantage of deferred compensation plans—401(k)s and Roths and so on. They put their money away, and they let it grow.

The reason people don't retire financially independent is that they spend everything that they earn. Then they start to get a little bit desperate, because they don't have much money saved up at the age of fifty, and they start to try to play makeup ball by throwing whatever money they have or that they can borrow into some get-rich-quick scheme, which inevitably fails. The only ones who get rich from get-rich-quick schemes are those who sell them. So people become desperate.

The fact is that a person who saves $100 a month and invests it in an index fund or a well-managed conservative mutual fund will find that it grows at about 8% to 10% per year over time, and, at $100 a month over the course of a person's working lifetime, they'll become a millionaire. The numbers are really interesting. They say of 100 people who start work today, one will be rich, four will be well-off, fifteen will be financially independent, and the other eighty will be either broke, dead, or still working when they reach retirement age.

Why is that? It's not because they didn't make enough money. I had a great experience some years ago. I was giving a seminar and talking about how anybody can become wealthy if they start early enough, work hard enough, stay late enough, and so on. People were gathered around me at the break asking question, and a mentally and physically challenged young man came up.

He shouted, "Mr. Tracy! Mr. Tracy!" The others quieted down. He said, "Can I be rich too?" All eyes swiveled toward me. He said, "I work in a group home. And we repair furniture. They pay us, and I save $100 every month. If I do that, can I become rich too?"

I had looked at these numbers the day before and had seen that if you saved $100 per month and invested it in a conservative mutual fund for your entire working life, it would be worth more than $1 million when you retired at the age of sixty-five. I repeated those numbers. I said, "Yes, if you were to save $100 a month throughout your career, when you reach the age of sixty-five, you will be a millionaire. You will be wealthier than all these other people walking around and driving cars and flying off on vacations. With few advantages in life, you will be a millionaire."

Remember that a person who starts early enough and saves long enough and doesn't touch the money gets into the miracle of compounding—time in the market. You don't have to be a company owner. You don't have to be an entrepreneur. You can just invest in other stocks and be a small owner of a small part of many different companies that are well-managed, well-run by experts, and you too can become financially independent.

Dan

The next myth is one that most everyone believes. Myth number four: Most wealthy people live in expensive neighborhoods, drive luxury cars, and spend lavishly. "The groundbreaking research of *The Millionaire Next Door* exploded this myth, showing how most wealthy people live in middle-class neighborhoods, drive standard cars, and are often more frugal. Then who lives in these high-priced places and drives these new luxury cars? Let's discuss the difference between wealth and income. Where do you strike a balance between these two ways of living?

Brian

There are three parts of life: you have your learning years, and then you have your earning years, and then you have your yearning years. Today, of course, we say that your learning years go on forever, but your earning years are where you work hard and accumulate money and put that money to work, so at a certain point you reach a crossover where your invested money is earning more than you are. That's the point where you start to gear down, and you can begin to gradually fade out of working for maybe five or ten years. Then you can just manage your money carefully and live comfortably for the rest of your life.

Most entrepreneurs have the characteristic of ambition, which is another way of saying that they're hungry, and the reason that they are hungry is that they came from backgrounds where they didn't have a lot. They say that whatever you felt you were most deprived of as a child is what you will strive for most as an adult. It's almost like a deficiency need. It's validated in psychology. They usually felt that they were deprived of enough money, so they are really hungry to get money. They find that starting a business and selling stuff and working hard is the way to get money.

The question is, when is the crossover time? A banker friend of mine was talking about an entrepreneur who had come in and wanted to buy an expensive house. My friend said that you can always tell when a business is going to get into trouble: the business finally starts to earn a profit, and the owner of the business decides now it's time to cut loose. They buy an expensive car. They finance it through the bank. They buy an expensive home. They finance it through the bank. And you can tell they're going to get into trouble, because they start to spend too soon.

Then, of course, recessions and depressions and ups and downs in industries and in the economy take place. The company takes a dip, the cash flow is cut off, and the person can't make their payments. The car company takes back the car, and the bank takes back the house. This bank always required a minimum of 20% deposit, so they had a very good collateral cushion. So if the person could come up with the money—which they would do by extracting it from their company—then they would lend them the money, and they would just take the house back in the next downturn.

My banker friend said the time to start buying the house, the time to start spending, is after you've gone well over the hump, and you're financially independent, and you can start investing your excess.

This brings us back to a little story about Warren Buffett. When he came back from college at Columbia University to Omaha, Nebraska, with his wife, he was able to buy this one little house. It cost $25,000 or so at the time. He still lives there today.

He's the third richest man in the world, according to *Forbes*, but he still lives in that little house, never went anywhere else. He said it's not a good idea to spend your money too soon, so he got into the habit of investing all of his money and never spending it. Today he's the most successful investor in history.

The critical thing is timing—when you have enough money put aside so that if you bought a home, if the whole world went to hell in a handbasket, you'd still be capable of making your payments, taking care of your standard of living, providing for your family. But if you do it too soon, you'll run the risk of having an unexpected event take place and losing it all.

Dan

Here's another myth that seems to be catching on, as evidenced by the rise in Internet gambling. Myth number five: You can get rich by playing the lottery or winning a jackpot at a casino. Brian, I know that you are passionate about this particular myth. Discuss why this is so pervasive and how one could take that same money spent on these sure-to-lose methods to become wealthy the scientifically proven way.

Brian

The something-for-nothing disease is like a cancer. It seduces very subtly, and one subtle way is with a dollar for a lottery ticket. Striving or trying to get something for nothing destroys the soul of the individual who does it. It is a cumulative disease. It starts to consume the mental and emotional body.

I just came back from Las Vegas. I was there for two days. I stayed in two casinos. I walked through the casinos back and forth for a substantial amount of time, because they design them that way. You can't get to your room without going through the casinos and past the gaming tables and slot machines. I never spent a quarter in Las Vegas, because it is fundamentally wrong in my philosophy. And it's not because of the amount of money involved. Intelligent people don't gamble, because they know that it's fundamentally wrong.

First of all, nobody ever wins in Las Vegas. If you win, you get photographed and banned from the casinos. It's not even a secret. If you're a professional gambler and you win, they soon photograph you. They can sit there in what they call "the eye in the sky," and they can watch you. If they see you winning money, they can start to check you out against all the other casinos. They check your photograph against Atlantic City, Monte Carlo. If you've won money in another casino, they all share the information.

Nobody wins money in Las Vegas. They only delay the amount that they lose. If you're lucky, you can take longer to lose all your money before you leave. But it still destroys the souls of the people.

I once read a travel article in which the author said, "I have been to hell and back in the last week, and it's a place called Las

Vegas in the Nevada desert." He said that he had seen "the most miserable and unhappy, unkempt, dirty, smoking, tractor-capped, undershirted people in the world, wander through the casinos and see overweight men and women gambling away their kids' lunch money, and their food money, and their toy money, and their bicycle money at the tables." He said, "And the looks on their faces are looks of despair because now they've put the money in, and they've lost the money. They can't get it back."

When you check in at a hotel there, they take the entire bill on your credit card, because they know that many customers aren't going to be able to pay when they leave. Friends of mine drove to Las Vegas from LA in a brand-new Cadillac and came back on a Greyhound bus with the suitcase gone, the car gone, everything gone.

Successful people do not gamble. They will take calculated risks where they can have a major influence on the outcome. They will select a product or service, and they will test it on a small scale. They will make careful investments to see how it works. They will do due diligence to make sure the money that they are putting out has the extremely high possibility of safe return.

Then look at the people who do gamble in these casinos. It's always poor people. Poor people gamble disproportionately more than wealthy people. People who could least afford to spend the money are the ones who are doing this fantasy football and all of this gambling. The amount that they lose is an amount that they cannot afford, because it comes directly out of the mouths of their children. It's money they cannot spend on food.

These people do not have excess money. It's not like they're making $10,000 a month and their expenses are $5000, so they've got $5000 to blow. They're making $2000 or $3000 a month and their expenses are $3500 a month, and they don't have the spare penny. They start to become desperate.

I've found that gamblers never lose. They always *almost won.* You ask a person, "How did you do in Las Vegas?" He'll say, "I almost won the big one. I almost won." "But I see you are taking the bus to work today." "Yes, I had to leave my car there. I had to get some cash. But I almost won this time. I'll win next time."

Before breakfast, they convince themselves of something that is totally impossible. They get up in the morning, and they go down with the idea that they're actually going to win back the money that they lost the night before.

My philosophy is, stay away from "something for nothing." When I was young, my mother told me, don't steal. Don't do anything illegal. Don't commit a crime. Most mothers told us that. So I never did, and I still don't. I told my kids, never do anything dishonest. Never commit a crime.

I pay my taxes to the penny. I got audited by the IRS some years ago, and after seven months of audit, they came back, and they said, "The Tracys are the kind of people the IRS really likes. They earn a high income; they pay every single penny of taxes that are required. They have not one single tax dodge or one single questionable deduction. They are completely honest about their taxes." You know what he said? "We will never be back."

They've never been back, because they know. They look at our tax returns, which are professionally done, and we never mess around with a penny. We hate taxes like everybody else, but it's not right to try to get something for nothing, to get money that you have not earned and don't deserve. That's why I'm opposed to gambling of any kind. It destroys the soul of the gambler.

THREE

The Science of Spending

Dan

As we begin to outline the specifics of the Science of Money, let's begin with what everyone does, whether they are poor, lower middle-class, middle-class, or rich: everyone spends. There are many people who never save, never invest, and some rare people who never incur debt, but everyone spends. But there is a science to spending: spending that is consistent with wealth, and spending that is consistent with a lack of wealth.

Brian, let's begin by describing most people's experience with spending, which often involves spending on what they want when they want it with no strategy or plan. Can you outline the typical day of an average middle-class person who feels that they have no money to save and how they spend their money, such as on a daily Starbucks, going out to lunch every day, impulse spending on clothes? Contrast this with a person who spends with a plan or a strategy.

Brian

Let's go back to where spending comes from. We are all creatures of habit: 95% of what we do is habitual. We do it regularly, and we do it automatically without thinking. When you're a child, your parents reward you with an allowance. It's a small allowance for doing or not doing something.

I can still remember my father suggesting that I save 10% of my meager little allowance when I was five or six years old. That, to me, was outrageous. I wanted to spend the money, and I wanted to spend it on candy. And so I would take my allowance and go to the store with my mother and I would buy candy. So what I did at a very young age was to associate getting money with candy, with having fun, with enjoyment, with pleasure. Spending money makes us happy.

As we get older, we have the same feeling. When we get money, the first thing we think of is, what can I buy with this money? How can I spend it to make me happy? That's why, if you go to a tourist resort, you'll find it's full of trinkets and trash. Streets lined with stores selling absolute trash, completely useless things. They sell it to people who are on vacation, and part of their vacation is to go up and down the streets, buying trinkets and trash.

If you ask a person what they would you do if they won the lottery, the first thing they talk about is what they're going to buy. You have to change your thinking about spending. And instead of thinking, "If I get money, I'm going to make myself happy by spending it," you have to think, "If I get money, I'm going to make myself happy by saving it."

What do most people do when they get money? I was in a restaurant the other day. The restaurant was jammed, which I couldn't understand, because it was Wednesday night. Well, it was payday, and the restaurant was full of people spending their money because their paychecks just hit their bank accounts that day. And they're out at expensive restaurants, spending with both hands. This is because of the association between getting money and spending it. And what happens is we put less and less thought into it. So much spending now is impulse spending. An enormous number of purchases happen when people buy unthinkingly. This is why stores are designed to have impulse purchases at the cash register, stuff that you don't really need or want, displayed seductively at the end of each aisle.

Dan

What is the difference between good spending and bad spending? For example, good spending is on things that appreciate in value, things that you can easily afford, things that can ultimately help you to produce more wealth in the long run. Bad spending is the opposite.

Brian

Time and money can be spent or invested. If you spend it, it's gone forever. If you invest it, you get a return on it. This is what people don't understand. The more time you invest in improving yourself and your earning ability early in your career, the more money you earn, and the more of that money that you keep, the more it grows.

There's a law of conservation in money. It says it's not how much you *make*, but how much you *keep* that determines your financial future. Good spending is where you get a return on your investment, you preserve it, you save it. Bad spending is where the money is gone forever and you can never recover it.

Dan

The entrepreneur Jim Rohn had a philosophy for wealth that we can paraphrase like this: "Do what you have to do as quickly as you can so you can do what you want to do for as long as you can." In other words, discipline yourself to do the things that might seem difficult in the short run so that in the long term you can live the life you want.

Describe how to relate this idea to spending. The idea is that during the early part of your life, your spending in done in a thrifty and strategic way; then, for the vast majority of your life, you will have the wealth to spend as you want. Whereas if you never discipline yourself in spending early in your life, you might struggle with spending everything you earn for the rest of your life.

Brian

Rich DeVos, one of the founders of Amway, used to say something similar: you do a lot of things that you don't necessarily want to do—get up in the morning, work hard all day long, study in the evenings, upgrade your skills. You do these things for a long time so that you can do all the things that you want to do for the rest of your life.

Many people try to have their cake and eat it too. They want to have fun, fun, fun, all the time. You have all these people saying, "Work should be fun and life should be fun!"

Denis Waitley, the writer and speaker, had this wonderful line. He said that most people spend their lives on things that are tension-relieving rather than on things that are goal-achieving.

Albert Gray, another thinker who spent more than twelve years trying to find the secret of success, finally found that it is very simple. He said successful people make a habit of doing what unsuccessful people don't like to do. What is it that unsuccessful people don't like to do? Well, it's the same thing that *successful* people don't like to do. They don't like to get up early, get started, plan their days, work hard, upgrade their skills, but they do it because they realize that is the price of success. If you don't pay it, if you don't sow, you don't reap. If you don't pay the price of success, then you will never have it.

There is a great tragedy called *hesitation*, where people *mean* to do something. They're always *going to*, but they hesitate and procrastinate. They never do anything.

In my program *Making a Lot of Money*, I ask, why is it that people don't make a lot of money if it's possible for everyone to retire financially independent? Number one, it never occurs to them. It never occurs to them that they could make a lot of money, because they've never grown up with anybody who is financially independent. They associate with people who spend everything that they earn. They think this is the way the world is. They go with the crowd, the herd instinct.

The second thing is, if it *does* occur to them, they put it off. They say, "Well, yes, I could be financially successful, but not now. I'll start in a week, a month, or a year."

The third thing that holds them back is fear of failure. "What if I save my money and I lose it or if it doesn't work out?" You avoid that by investing your money very carefully, investing with experts. Never try to make a big kill or a big score. Always get lots of information.

Sadly, another reason is that many people have this fear: "If I set a goal of being financially successful, I'll be criticized by my friends." The answer for this is, don't tell them anything. Just keep your plans and your goals to yourself.

Finally, get started. Do the first thing that you need to do: open up a private bank account. Open up a Financial Freedom account, and put every spare penny you can into this account for as long as you can. The most remarkable things happen.

We know that spending becomes automatic. How do you stop spending? The first thing is, you start to keep track of your spending. If you go for debt consolidation treatment, the first thing they have you do is to sit down and make a list of every single expenditure down to the penny. And you have to write it down. You cannot spend it, on a credit card or in cash, without writing it down.

There are some very good apps to help you track your spending. The very fact of taking the time to think through how much you're spending causes you to be more and more conscious of how much you *are* spending. And it often causes you *not* to spend.

My friend David Bach, author of *The Automatic Millionaire*, talked about the latte factor: if you spend $5 on a latte each day and then you stop and you save that money, that's $25 a week, $100 a month. Accumulated over time, it could make you wealthy.

Another thing that I learned when I started studying self-made millionaires is that they never buy new cars. I was having this discussion with some wealthy people the other day who had learned this in my programs. They buy two-year-old cars, good-quality two-year-old cars, that are in great shape, checked out by a mechanic, and then they drive them forever. But the cars have lost all their depreciation, so you can buy a $55,000 car probably for $35,000.

I had dinner a couple of nights ago with one of the senior marketing executives of Lexus. He was saying that Lexus has brought in a recertification program. If you lease the car for two years and give it back, Lexus will recertify it with a five-year warranty and resell it. People could then buy that car and drive it forever. So that's what I do. I wait till I find a Lexus that's virtually brand-new, because it's been taken such good care of, and then get it recertified, which means it's been checked out from bumper to bumper. Then you just drive it forever, and you can save.

Let's say you save $10,000 on buying a new car. If you invest that $10,000 in property or in a good index fund, over the course of the three, or five, sometimes ten years that you drive the car, that money can double and triple. That can turn into a piece of property or a down payment on a piece of property. You may be able to put a down payment on a condo or an apartment and then rent that out. Then the renter pays for all the interest and payments, plus you get a return on your investment.

If you start doing that on a regular basis, it becomes quite astonishing. Spending money that continues to grow, investing money that continues to grow, that's good spending. Bad spending is when the money is gone forever.

Dan

Which categories might one want to eliminate from one's spending plan if one is serious about building wealth?

Brian

First, you realize that there are fixed expenses, like rent, cars, and so on. So you live in a smaller place. The Warren Buffett model: he lived in a small house when he was starting off, and he still lives there today. If Warren can do it, you can do it as well. Live in a smaller place so you can pay lower rent.

It has to do Parkinson's law: expenses rise to meet income. When most people have their incomes go up, they move to a bigger place that costs more. And it's bigger, so they buy more furniture, 80% of which they never use. Stay in a smaller place and take that additional money and save it, put it away, invest it. Remember: only money that is growing and eventually giving you a return is ever going to be of any value to you.

I had an experience many years ago, back in the '80s. I was doing a real estate development, a small one, and there was a notice that there was a condominium complex where they were selling off the individual units. You could buy a unit for $1250 and then make monthly payments. I went to look at it: $1250 was about a $30,000–35,000 unit. I didn't know anything about investing, but I could come up with $1250. I think I put it on a credit card.

I bought this little apartment, and then I found out that they were renting the apartments in this complex at about $275 a month. I put mine up for rent in the local paper for $250 a month and immediately got a tenant. It was a single woman with two young children. She paid me $250 a month, and I was paying $275 or $300 a month in payments. So I lost money for the first six months, and then I raised her rent, and then I broke even. Six months later, I raised her rent another $25.

Soon I got it up to the point where she was paying about $350–375 a month. She stayed there year after year. She actually stayed there and raised her kids. They went up through school, up through college. She stayed there for ten years, and I regularly raised the rent. At a certain point I was getting $1250 net income back on that apartment. And remember: my initial investment was only $1250! When she announced that her kids had grown up and finished school and that she was going to move out, I sold the apartment.

In retrospect, I think selling then was probably one of the dumbest things that I've ever done. That condo was paying me 100% per year in return on my initial investment of $1250. A 100% return. What if I had bought one apartment like that each year? Every time you buy an apartment, the banks will lend you more money to buy more apartments, since you've demonstrated success in this area.

That's one of the things that Warren Buffett did. He bought companies that threw off cash flow, and he took that cash flow to buy more companies that threw off cash flow. It was like a little hose, and then pretty soon like a fire hose, and now he's generating $25 billion a year. That's $2 billion a month in cash flow, which he can then use along with more money from the bank. The banks will lend him anything he wants.

If I had done the same thing, I would own apartment buildings, but I was too young to even think about it. Anybody can do that. If you can just find one apartment or condo that's for sale nearby, and make sure it's all cleaned up and do a little bit of homework and make a down payment, you start your real estate empire.

Dan

That's a great way to spend on something important that can also provide a return.

In which categories might one want to consider increasing one's spending if one is serious about building wealth, for example: ongoing education, high-quality business equipment to increase efficiency, etc.?

Brian

It's the Earl Nightingale rule: invest 3% of your income back into yourself, improving your skills. As soon as I heard it, I began to practice it, and now I say there's no limit on how much you can expend to improve your skills.

Some years I was spending thousands of dollars. I took a two-year executive MBA at the university. It cost thousands of dollars, but it was a fantastic investment.

I had a gentleman come up to me recently and he said, "I came to your seminar about eight years ago and you taught that 3% rule: invest 3% back in yourself." At the time he was living at home with his mother. He was making $20,000 a year and had an old car.

I said, "Three percent of $20,000 is $600." He bought a couple of audio programs from Nightingale-Conant, our dear friend, and some books, and went to one seminar. That year his income went from $20,000 to $30,000, and that's a 50% increase, which is what I said would happen. And he said he could directly relate this increase to what he learned in those programs.

So now he's making $30,000, and 3% of $30,000 is $900. The next year he spent $900, and his income went to $50,000. The following year he spent again, $1500, and his income went to $80,000. He saw that this really works. He increased it to 5%, and that year his income almost doubled. So he decided to go all in. In his fifth year he spent 10% of his income, and his income doubled. And then he did it again.

I asked how he was doing now. He said he passed a million dollars this year and that he still invests 10% back into himself. I said, "Ten percent, that's $100,000 a year; how on earth do you do that?" He said, "It's hard. I used to go to seminars. Now I hire those seminar speakers to come in and spend a day with me coaching. I have special coaches. I have advisors. I travel to international conferences. I have my own learning library, with television sets and videos and DVDs and audios and books. It's hard to spent $100,000, but my income just keeps going up by 10, 20, 30% a year, and these expenses are all tax-deductible."

It really works. *HR* magazine looked at how much return companies nationwide got back on their investment in training. It ranged anywhere from $22 to $33 per dollar that they invested.

I spoke to a very wealthy woman just a couple of days ago. She said, "I bought one of your audio programs from Nightingale-Conant twenty-two years ago. My husband and I listened to it over and over again. We had been married for about three or four years, we had one child, and we started saying, 'I like myself and I can earn a million dollars a year. I earn a million dollars a year.' So we started repeating these affirmations, and you know what? Within five years my husband's on Wall Street making a million dollars a year. Because of that one audio program we became rich."

I've had people who, from one book, one audio program, one course, one seminar, one coaching program all increased their income the next year. I have a friend who paid $100,000 to get a personal coach for an entire year and increased their income by a million dollars the following year.

So the very best investment, the very best expenditure, is to spend on yourself. Spend on making yourself better. What if somebody came to you with an investment and said, "I'd like you to invest in this. It looks like a really good investment. It's got great potential for the future"? And you looked at it and said, "No, I'm not going to invest in that. I just don't think it has any future. I don't think it's going to be a successful investment, so it would be a waste of my money."

How does this apply to investing in yourself? At an unconscious level, people who do not invest in themselves have feelings of undeservingness, self-doubt, lack of belief in themselves. They've made a decision that they're not worth it, that investing in themselves is a waste of money, because they have no future.

You can always tell people who have given up on themselves, because they don't invest in themselves. Many people would be shocked to hear that. Yet it is true. Because here's one of the greatest discoveries of all time: you can only tell what your beliefs are by looking at what you do. Especially what you do when you have a choice. You always choose what it is in alignment with your deepest, innermost beliefs and values.

So if you're given a choice to buy a latte or to buy a CD, if you're given a choice to go on a vacation or to attend a seminar, and you choose the fun, you've chosen the tension-relieving activity, you're saying that this is more important to you than your own personal growth and development.

Whatever you do repeatedly becomes a habit. Pretty soon you get into a habit of never investing in yourself, and as far as you're concerned, it's automatic. In fact, if somebody comes to you, and says, "You should get a copy of this book—it's in paperback now, it's only $12"—you'll actually get angry with that person for suggesting that you move out of your comfort zone. You'll become angry and resistant. You'll actually be negative toward the person who is suggesting that you invest in yourself.

Louise Hay, the spiritual author, once said that the greatest problem of the human race is the feeling "I'm not good enough. I'm not good enough." It's of no value for me to invest in myself, because I'm not good enough, and it won't do any good because I have no future." You can say, "I've never made that decision." No, but you made it by default.

That's like saying, "I never made the decision to be unfit." But if you decide not to exercise, you have made the decision to be unfit by default. If you choose not to engage in developing yourself, you've made a decision to fail at life, because if you're not working on yourself, you have no future.

Another way to think about this is to ask if you were a stock, would you invest in yourself? Would you buy any? That's a shocker too. Do you think you're a growth stock? Are you a stock that widows and orphans could invest in, because your value is going up and up?

Many years ago I got into financial trouble. I was broke and I needed money. A friend of mine, a very smart guy, said, "I'll lend you some money if you'll give me 20% of your profits for the future." My business had no profits at that time, and I said, "Sure, absolutely, no problem." He saw that I was a growth stock, so he gave me $10,000 or $20,000, which I needed to save my business. Then I started to make a profit. My profits were $10,000 and then $20,000 and then $30,000 and I'd give him 20%.

Eventually I bought my soul back from him. I gave him $40,000 rather than having him carry interest on my income for the indefinite future. That was the smartest 100% return on his money that I had ever given anybody.

Think about that. Are you a growth stock? Are you the kind of stock that makes me say, "I'll invest in you. I'm going to get rich because you're increasing your value so much"?

Dan

For entrepreneurs and small business owners, what are some of the biggest spending mistakes that most business owners make?

Brian

The number one rule in starting a business is preserve cash, preserve cash, preserve cash. Which means, never buy when you can lease. Never lease when you can rent. Never rent when you can borrow. Never borrow long-term if you can borrow short-term. Therefore, you never lease offices, you rent them, even if you have to move. You buy used furniture. I learned this. There's used furniture out there for ten cents on the dollar, and it's fine for now.

I remember many years ago I was asked to set up the distribution of a line of Japanese vehicles for western Canada. I found some warehouses in an old warehouse district. I bought used furniture, and I set up the offices and parts department and everything else. Then my Japanese counterparts came out from Tokyo to take a look at the facilities. The manager walked in and said, "Aha! Cheap offices. Cheap furniture. I like this. Cheap offices, big profits. We like our distributors to make big profits."

He said that he saw distributors all the time who go out and borrow a bunch of money, get brand-new offices, pay top dollar for first-class, new everything. He said that they almost all went broke before they made enough profit. "Cheap offices, big profit," he said. I never forgot that.

It's a very important lesson, and it was learned by many companies that went broke during the dot-com collapse. These people moved into first-class office premises. They bought first-class everything, and then they ran out of cash.

What you want to do is preserve cash. Never spend it if you possibly can. Save the money. Borrow or rent on short term. Even get it from your friends if necessary, but preserve cash, because cash is like oxygen to the brain. If you have cash, you can survive. If you run out of cash, the business can turn over like a ship in the ocean and sink immediately. A business that's been in business for 100 years can die if it runs out of cash.

So preserve cash. That's what I've learned, because I've made all the same mistakes.

Dan

Brian, to wrap up, are there three keys or principles to never forget on this topic of spending?

Brian

Write everything down. The most important thing is to create a financial plan, and write everything down in detail. Write down what you think things are going to cost and then double check. Many companies have gone broke because they underestimated the cost of essential furniture, essential raw materials, essential people, essential advertising; they didn't do their due diligence. These words, *due diligence*, have become my favorite words because of the mistakes I've made in business. People make financial commitments and decisions without getting enough information.

Do a thorough financial plan. Committing things to paper forces you to think about them very carefully. Creating a budget is something many entrepreneurs hate to do because they are not detail oriented people. Then find someone else. Get an accountant, somebody who loves detail, and then make a list of everything that you're possibly going to need to do your business. And then shop around and double-check and pick up the phone and double-check, and keep your expenses as low as possible.

The second thing is to defer big expenditures as long as possible. If you think you need a whole new computer setup or something like that, put it off for a month, put it off for two months, it's no emergency. You'll find that people who sell these things will do everything possible to get you to hurry up. If they're commissioned, they get the commission when the check clears.

In both personal and business finance, you'll find that if you wait thirty days to make any kind of decision, you'll probably not make it at all. We have a tendency to think, "Oh, that's a great idea: a new car or a new computer or something else." But you put thirty days in before the decision, and you'll be amazed at how much better your decision is and how rarely you decide to buy it. I've decided to buy things and given myself that thirty-day fuse. At that point I didn't even remember why I'd been interested in buying those things. So give yourself as much time as possible.

The third thing is to get advice from more experienced people or people who are really careful with money. I have some good friends who are just very, very careful with money. When I ask them about certain expenditures, they have all kinds of great ideas. Don't buy this. Don't buy it here. You can get it cheaper there. You don't really need it. You can borrow here. You can do something else there.

Sometimes you can lease facilities. Jeff Bezos, the founder of Amazon, has just become the fourth richest man in the world. He had all this cloud computing capacity for Amazon and actually had an overabundance, so he began to rent it out. Now he rents out cloud computing capacity for thousands, tens of thousands of companies. He's making billions of dollars a year.

So if you and I started our own business, we could just go to Amazon, hook up, buy everything that we need. Also, Amazon will sell anything for others, as will eBay, so you don't need to have your own store. You don't even need your own website. There are other companies that will set up websites for you; for instance, Google will do that. They'll set up your entire website so that your goods or services can become available to everybody in the world.

These are all ways of putting off expenditures until you absolutely have to make them. It should be at the point where you are so big and the savings are so great from making this expenditure that it will more than pay for itself.

FOUR

The Science of Debt

Another area of the Science of Money that the vast majority of people experience is debt. It's common to every income class and every age bracket. Yet did you know that not all debt is created equal? Did you know that the wealthy incur very different kinds of debt than the vast majority of people in the lower and middle classes? What is the best way to get out of the hole of consumer debt?

Dan

Brian, let's begin by having you describe your own experience with debt both as a young man and now as a wealthy business owner. Did you ever struggle with it? If yes, how did you finally get out of the hole of consumer debt, and if not, what principles did you live by in order to remain debt-free?

Brian

When I finished high school, I did not graduate, so I could only work at laboring jobs. So there was no real problem about getting into debt, because no one would lend me any money. I had no credit cards. I had only enough money in the bank to be able to pay my expenses, and I had to pay for everything with cash.

I worked for several years. I traveled overseas, I visited eighty countries by shank's pony, as it was called, hitchhiking, traveling on buses and trucks, stopping to work here and there to make enough money to go on. Even when I started to make better money in sales, it was all payable pretty much in cash because I was working overseas at that time. I had money in the bank, but never any debt.

Time passed, and I started my own business. I joke that when you start your own business, you learn how to sell again. I sold my house, I sold my car, I sold my furniture, I sold everything I owned, plus I used all of the savings that I had been able to accumulate. I rented a small office, because when you start your own business, unless you're starting with a lot of money, you can go straight off a cliff.

There's a rule that everything costs twice as much as you expect and takes three times as long, so if you think you're going to break even in six months, it's going to be twelve months. Everything is going to cost more, things that you never imagined. Even when you make your very best budget and gross up by 50–100%, you're still going to be surprised.

As a result, I got deeply into debt. I had borrowed some money. I had ordered supplies: printing, mailing, furniture, utilities, supplies from different companies, and I thought everything was going great. I went through all the money, and then the money was gone. That's when they started ringing my doorbell, phoning me, harassing me, all of that. It was calls, bills, harassers all the time, and I was really panicking.

We had no money for anything. We were living in a rented house and I was scrambling the whole time, so I had to retrench. When you start a new business, lots of people borrow from their friends, borrow from their relatives, run up every credit card to the maximum. In my case, I had to borrow against my car and all kinds of things.

I sat down and realized that I was going to have to dig myself out of this debt or go bankrupt. I thought that if I worked really hard, I could do it. The first thing was to go to my bank. It was something like a one-year revolving loan, which had to be paid off. I had borrowed from a bank when I had a house. Now I had no house, but I still owed bank payments.

Then I read that if you keep the loan current with regard to interest, it's not on the books of the bank as a bad loan. They don't have to report it, so they don't have to seize property or assets. I went to my bank manager, and said, "Look, I cannot make principal payments, but I can make interest payments on this loan until my business recovers, which it should in the next three to six months." He said, "As long as you can make interest payments, Brian, then it's not a problem with me, because it appears as a good loan."

Then I went to each of my creditors, and said, "Look, I've got this problem: I owe all this money and I cannot pay you off, but I will pay you a small amount each month as a sign of good faith, and I will pay it all off in six to twelve months if you'll just roll with me for a while." Every one of them, without exception, said, "OK, if you'll make us a good-faith payment every month, we'll roll with you." I owed thousands of dollars, and I'd be paying $50 a month.

I went back to work, and within six months business had turned around. I was able to pay off all of my debts, got all my loans current, and got everything else into shape. It was a terrible one and a half years, but I never went into debt again

That's why we said previously that it's absolute nonsense to say, "Don't spend your own money when you start your own business," because to get started you often have to spend every penny that you can beg, borrow, steal—everything that you own or ever accumulated. According to *Forbes* magazine, 80% of new businesses go broke within two years. They say every new business is a race against time: do you figure out how to make more money than it's costing you before you run out of money?

Imagine a plane that's in a dive. It's going toward the ground, and it's going faster and faster toward the ground. This is what's happening to your business. You must find a way to pull it out of the dive, where you start to actually bring in more money than it's costing you. You just barely pull it out of the dive, and then you start to climb again. The rule in business is, it takes you two years to break even, and two more years to pay back the amount of money that you borrowed in the first two years. No business, according to Peter Drucker, makes a profit until four years out. If you plan for anything other than that, you're crazy.

Someone told me that it's two, two, and three: two years to break even, two more years to get even with your debts, then three more years to burst into the open sky and start to make a profit. So it's good to have enough money to carry yourself for two years, or you'll crash.

When I heard that, I said, "That's nonsense, that's not going to happen to me. I'm different, I'm superior." It took seven years. And everybody I ever speak to you talks about that seven-year rule. It costs twice as much and takes three times as long as you thought; it takes two years to break even, two years to pay back, seven years total to make a profit. When a person has finally become a successful entrepreneur, they've been through all those phases.

When you see these stories about people who become wealthy very quickly in Silicon Valley, it's only happening because of absolute miracles in technology. We're living through an incredible age, but remember there are 30 million businesses in the U.S., and of those, there are probably 100,000 in high-tech, while most of the other 29 million are small to medium-sized businesses with people trying to sell stuff and stay alive.

Dan

Brian, we've alluded to the fact that there are different kinds of debt. There's what we might call good debt and bad debt. Please clearly describe the difference between these two kinds of debt and give us some specific examples.

Brian

We've talked about this before: good debt is debt that pays for itself. For instance, if you buy products to resell, if you invest in advertising that brings you customers to buy your product, if you train your staff so they can sell more of your stuff, if you invest in traveling to meet with clients and you have to put it on a credit card, this is all money that has an expected return on investment. You expect to get back far more than you pay.

Bad debt is where you spend the money, and it's gone forever, like on furniture. We just closed our main offices because we've reorganized our business. We opened offices that are twice the size but are much better designed for us as a digital marketing business. Our employees wanted open space, modern furniture. Previously I had traditional offices, traditional desk furniture. I'd paid tens of thousands of dollars for beautiful furniture, mahogany desks, all top-notch.

Now it was time to dispense with all of this, and we asked if anybody would like to buy it. They didn't even want it for free. This is what you might call bad debt. In a couple of cases, we had to agree to pay to ship it over to them so they would accept it for free. The whole office was basically stripped down to nothing, and we didn't make a penny on tens of thousands of dollars' worth of stuff. That's bad debt, there's no return on it.

We also made the mistake, as many companies do, of ordering too much product, because you think you're going to sell so much, and then you don't, but you still have to pay for the product. You've got thirty- or sixty-day payment plans, and a warehouse full of product, and the products are not moving. Many companies go bankrupt because they've stocked too much inventory. That's another example of bad debt.

Why would you do that? It's because you can get lower prices if you buy in volume. But it's much better at the beginning to buy smaller quantities, even though you pay higher prices and have lower profit. At least you're not exposed; your cash is not gone, and you don't end up with a warehouse full of dead stock. Dead stock kills businesses, so that's another place where you can get bad debt. You've got this stock, and if you don't convert it into sales very quickly, it can drag your business down. That kind of bad debt is a major reason companies go broke.

Dan

Let's talk a little bit about some forms of consumer bad debt. We've talked a bit about credit cards, with their high interest rates. Extended car loans are very big right now; we can go out to seventy-two months or more. And there are forms of home equity lines of credit. Can you address these and how they can be temptations for bad debt if they're not used properly?

Brian

The credit card industry makes its profit on interest payments and the interest payments can run 18–23% or even more: there are all kinds of hidden payments, late payment fees, and so on. So the only way to use a credit card is to pay if off every month. Credit card debt is the highest-cost debt that you can possibly have, and they make billions of dollars on it. That's one of the worst forms of personal debt.

Extended car loans are another kind of bad debt. Basically you're buying too much car. You should be able to pay off a car in thirty-six months, so if it takes any longer than that, you're buying too much car. Buy less car. Get your ego under control.

Regarding a home equity line of credit—it doesn't cost anything if you don't use it, so they like you to use it. I have a home equity line of credit, but it basically costs $250 a year. A home equity line of credit is really a good cushion if you're running a business and they will not give your company a line of credit. You could use a home equity line if you have one. Just make sure that the carrying costs are very low and read the fine print; those details are important.

I want to touch again on buying furniture on credit cards or buying furniture on credit plans. When I was young and foolish, I went to a furniture store and they had all these great deals, so I furnished my entire apartment. They had their own financing plan—just sign here, sign there. It was 24% a year. I had no idea that it was almost like Mafia rates, but that's how they made their money. They sold used furniture, and they financed it themselves at 24%. You had to make a down payment. I didn't realize that until I started to get the bills. I thought, "Oh my God, if I carry this stuff for three years, I'll end up having paid twice as much," so I paid it all down.

Whenever you get into a financial commitment, take the time to bring the documents home and sit down, read them, and go through them, bit by bit. If you don't understand something, demand a full explanation, because some of these documents are written by geniuses to confuse average people, so you won't understand what this subclause means. For instance, with credit cards, it might say 0% interest for the first six months, but that's only if you pay off 100% each month or if you carry a $2000 balance. Read the fine print, because you can get trapped. It can say 0% or 1% per month, or 12% per year, and so on.

Also, be very careful when they call you on the phone and make special offers through your credit cards, or your telephone plans, or anything else. These special offers on the phone are usually outrageously priced and include 50–80% commission for the people phoning you. They try to get you into stuff that you have no need of: extra insurance, extended warranties on cars, or technical equipment like computers and cell phones. These can be outrageously expensive and are of no value to you at all.

Dan

Can you clarify how each of these forms of debt can be used responsibly? For example, credit cards that are paid in full each month, lines of credit for business investment, shorter car loans that are easily affordable, etc. Let's emphasize that for those who don't have the discipline to use them responsibly, it is better to stay away from these forms of debt entirely.

Brian

This is going to depend a lot on your credit rating and your savvy, but there are three different recommendations. One is called *debt consolidation*. Debt consolidation means they put all your debts together with one company, and then you only owe money and make payments to that one company. Although there are a lot of companies that do this, you have got to be very careful, because they make big commissions on consolidating your debt. The companies that do this make a big profit. Almost all people who do this consolidation get into trouble. It can seem like they've gotten off easy, and as a result they begin again spending beyond their means. This leads to another default and another debt consolidation.

Another way, suggested by financial author Dave Ramsey, is to make a list of everything that you owe and pay off the smallest debt first. It is a good idea, because it gives you psychological momentum to pay off a small debt and cross it off your list, and pay off the next debt and cross that off your list.

Another recommendation I especially like is to pay off the highest interest debt first. Look at your credit cards: some are charging you 18%, some 23%, some 30%. Pay off the ones that are charging the highest interest first. Dedicate all of your savings to that one. Some people say, pay a little bit here and a little bit there. I would say, pay minimum payments on the others just to keep them current. They cannot come after you as long as you're making the minimum payments.

Once you've decided to get out of debt, there's a series of strategies that you can use. One is to begin saving your money. The rule, George Clason's rule, is to pay yourself first, which means that you save 10% or more of your income every month. But if you're deeply in debt, you have to start off small, and there are two ways to do this.

Let us say that you are in debt and you want to save money as well as get out of debt, but you can't save 10% per month. What I recommend is to start saving 1% and live on the other 99%. People are creatures of habit, so if you can, take 1% and save it at the beginning of each month, right off the top of your paycheck. You'll be quite comfortable living on 99%. Second month, save 2%; third month, save 3%.

Over the course of a year you can build up to saving 12%, and the tightening of your standard of living will be so small that you won't even notice it. It may be one latte a day. Then write down everything that you spend, so that you are cognizant of the fact that you're spending this money. Just writing it down will cause you not to spend it. Then you save that money. As you begin to save money and begin to develop a Financial Freedom account, something remarkable happens to your debts. Your mind space changes, your attitude toward debt changes, and you stop accumulating debt.

It's often recommended that you cut up your credit cards and pay cash for everything. I don't recommend that. It's a bit severe, because it's quite inconvenient to be getting cash all the time. I carry three credit cards. I have all kinds of credit cards that I never use, but I only use three plus a debit card, and I keep everything paid off every single month. If you don't, it can accumulate—and quickly. I learned the hard way. I carry no credit card debt at all.

The other thing about getting out of debt is that as you begin to save 1% a month, you'll find yourself spending less and less on debt. It may take you two to three years, but then you'll reach the point where you're out of debt completely, and then you never get back in. I've spoken to countless people who have done this, and it changes their lives.

When you're in debt, it causes you to feel inferior, anxious, insecure, and negative. Let's look at the difference between two people talking. One has money in the bank, and the other is in debt. The person with money in the bank is more confident, more positive, more outspoken. The person who owes money feels a little bit inferior. They're more cautious, they're more obsequious toward the person who's got money. When you get out of debt, it transforms your personality. Most people who've done it never get back in.

You can do it, just 1% a month. And if you practice some of the other things we talk about in terms of increasing your income, it will start to go up. As your income goes up, you save that money instead of spending it and pay down your debt.

Dan

Brian, are you a believer in carrying a mortgage rather than paying it off right away? Is it a good idea to accelerate payments?

Brian

There are many schools of thought. We have a 3% mortgage on our house, and there's no place that you could invest money at 3% interest. If you have a low interest rate, it is much better to carry the house mortgage, especially in today's real estate market, as home prices are going up faster than the payments that you're making. So it is an investment, because it actually is increasing in value.

Another strategy is to pay off your mortgage completely or make extra payments. Let's say you get bonuses, sales commissions, or other chunks of cash: you can use those to pay against your mortgage. Some people say if you make two principal payments a month, you can pay off the mortgage in half the time.

That is a good strategy for people, because it does not cut into their lifestyle, although it requires a little bit of sacrifice. But it takes a thirty-year mortgage down to fifteen years, and then you own the property free and clear.

Dan

Today another big topic of debate is college loans. Let's discuss college debt. Some look at it as bad debt, others as good debt, because you're investing in yourself for the future.

Brian

I was just doing some in-depth reading on the returns on investment for various courses of study. The STEM courses—science, technology, engineering, and math—pay the most. They start at about $76,000 per year when you get out of school, and they go up to about $136,000 a year for petroleum engineers.

Many courses people take are useless, and when they come out they're unemployable. In the last year, 54% of college students were still unemployed one year after graduating from college, because the courses that they took were useless. They're not taking courses that increase their earning ability or enable them to get results that a company's willing to pay for. So what are they borrowing the money for?

It's like going to Las Vegas. If you're borrowing the money to buy a home there—and Las Vegas prices are going up 7–8% now after the recession—that's a good investment. If you're borrowing the money to go to the casino, that's not a good investment. People who are borrowing money to take useless courses are making a bad investment, because half of them will be working at minimum wage jobs for the next couple of years.

Eighty percent of college students never work in their field of major after they leave college. They'll never go back to it, because the courses that they took are basically entertainment courses. They're excuses to stay at the university and play with your friends, and have parties, and drink, and everything else. That's the difference between good college debt and poor college debt.

A person who borrows to go to medical school or to get an engineering degree is very smart, because they're going to be able to pay off the whole darn thing in two to three years. If you don't have a good income because you've got a minimum wage job because you took a useless course, then that's very bad debt. There are some people in their thirties who still cannot buy a house, they can't get credit for a car, they can't start a business, and they can't get a bank loan, because this college debt overhangs them like an avalanche.

Dan

Does it matter what school we invest in? Would it be better to go to an Ivy League school, or is somebody better off going to any accredited college program?

Brian

Fortunately, President Obama is insisting that, for the first time in history, colleges actually report the amount that their graduates are earning one year, two years, five years, ten years after graduating in a particular course of study. Those figures become publicly available. The colleges and universities are fighting it screaming and kicking, because they don't want people to know these numbers. Fortunately, again, if you go on Google, there are some very good assessments of how much a person is likely to make with a degree from a particular college.

I just read a study on this, where they looked at the top ten best universities and the worst ten in terms of return on investment. If you go to Harvard, for example, and you take a degree in law, or finance, or economics, your chances of getting a good, high-paying job quickly are very high. Harvard is one of the best. Yale happens to be one of the worst.

If you have a degree from a prestigious university, but it's in useless subjects, it's not going to help you very much to get a high-paying job. All this information is universally available. You need to do your homework. They show you what the lowest-paying faculties are and what the highest-paying faculties are. It's your job to do some research before you get into debt. Just as if you were going to invest in a company, you have to be sure that the company is going to have high levels of sales and profitability, and will pay dividends to justify the investment in the first place.

Dan

Do you think that people should be contributing to a 401(k) and/or contributing to a savings account if they have any bad consumer debt? Why or why not? In other words, if they have credit card debt and they're contributing to a 401(k), is that a smart thing to do concurrently: try to pay down a little bit here and pay the 401(k) over there? Or should you just get all the debt paid off before you put one penny in the 401(k)?

Brian

Again it depends upon your individual situation—how much you're earning, how much discretionary cash you have. A 401(k) is generally considered to be one of the best investments because it's completely pretax, and it's often matched. That is, if you put in $1, your employer will put in $0.50 or $1. You get a two-for, and that money can accumulate.

Most people later on in life say the biggest regret they have is they did not start putting money into a 401(k) early enough. They should have done it right from the very beginning of their careers. They could have ended up financially independent.

Dan

Do you believe in the concept described by Debt-Reduction and Financial Freedom expert, Dave Ramsey, of putting as much money toward debt and utilizing the snowball method to get out of debt completely? Do you think it's a good idea to set a goal of being totally debt-free? Or does such frugal living take away from the creativity, and sometimes the leverage, required to be successful on a larger scale?

Here I'm thinking of the entrepreneur who starts a business by mortgaging the house or maxing out a couple of credit cards versus the person who spends years getting out of debt but as a result never gets that business idea off the ground. Is there a way to strike a balance here?

Brian

The most important requirement for success in life, especially business, is self-discipline; hard work and self-discipline. Dave Ramsey's approach requires tremendous self-discipline. Self-discipline is manifested in delayed gratification. Successful people are those who are able to delay gratification in the short term in order to enjoy financial security in the long term.

Ramsey's approach almost forces you into a form of boot camp. You have to be very disciplined about your finances. Since your habits are going to determine your success, if you're very disciplined about paying things off and getting out of debt and being very strict on yourself, you're probably going to be a vastly better business person, you're going to make better decisions, you're going to be more thorough and careful about taking on debt and expenses, so I think it would be to your benefit.

Everything that helps a person to develop self-discipline and to delay gratification in the short term builds their character, builds their persistence, their tenacity, their thoroughness, and builds their best qualities overall. It's a really good idea if you can do it, but it's very hard to do. That's why most people don't do it. Dave Ramsey, I think, is being very clear and very strict. If you're serious, then go whole hog. It's just as if you're going to lose weight, then you cut back to 2000 calories a day, and you stay at 2000 calories a day for one year, and you don't have exceptions.

A good friend of mine was overweight. I've known him for thirty years. He'd been overweight the whole time, about thirty to forty pounds. Then I saw him a couple of months ago, and he was trim, almost like an athlete, and I said, "I've known you all your life; what on earth happened?"

He said he'd gotten one of those calorie counter apps, and it tells you you're only allowed 2000 calories a day. You have to mark down every single food and the number of calories, and at a certain point it says, stop, you cannot have any more calories today. If you eat all your calories by noon, then you're going to starve until breakfast the next morning. He said you only have to do that a couple of times before you start spreading the calories across the whole day. Final calories are 6 or 7 o'clock in the evening, so you can get to sleep. He said that if you're strict with yourself, it doesn't take long to get into the habit of consuming 2000 calories.

The average adult consumes 3000 calories a day, so if you take in 3000 and you burn up 4000, then you're going to lose 1000 calories a day, and over time, gradually, the extra weight goes away. It's the most amazing thing, but you have to be really strict with yourself. That's what the Ramsey method is. Be really strict with yourself, develop the habit of being frugal and careful with money. If you do this for a year or two, you'll be careful with money for the rest of your life.

Dan

In terms of a business, you've talked about your own experience in the early days, and you hear how this is very common with entrepreneurs: they max out every credit card, they go through the home equity, and so forth. There are some people who say it's possible to start and run a business debt-free from the beginning without having to go to those methods. Is it realistic to be debt-free when starting a business?

Brian

Yes. The most important key to success in business is sales. If you have a business where you can start selling stuff that you get on consignment, then you can actually launch your business today and be generating revenues before you pay anything. There are many websites where you can buy products wholesale, and then you can develop your own website and sell them, so you don't buy them from the supplier until you have the sale in hand.

The most popular of these is MLM—multilevel marketing—or network marketing. You can start in network marketing with a very small investment for a sample kit. From then on you take your samples and sell the product, get the order, then buy the product, deliver it, and make a profit in between. The critical thing is sales ability, so you could actually start with nothing and sell your way to success.

It's called bootstrapping, where you start with your own money and you grow out of your own profits. It's a slower way to start a business, but it's often the best way, because if you don't have any extra money, you are forced to sell immediately, you are forced to be creative, to fall back on hard work and self-discipline. What killed all those dot-com dot-bombs was they had too much money too soon, and they burned through all of it.

In fact, I just read of a company that had raised $400 million in venture capital in Silicon Valley. Before they ever made a sale, they were out of money, and the investors lost it all—$400 million. They had what seemed like a great idea, but they just never got around to selling the product. Start off by selling the product first. Sometimes you can sell products for another company. You sell for them and make commissions on the sale. You can start your business if you can sell. That's the only way that I know of to do it, and it's a very popular way.

Dan

The final idea for this chapter, Brian, comes to the point where someone has paid off all their debt; they've finally gotten all the weight off. We know how many people get weight off, but the weight comes right back on again. The question here is, how do you get to a point where an unexpected huge expense doesn't throw the whole thing off again so you're back in debt? How many months of savings would you recommend someone have in a bank account to keep an unsustainable expense from throwing their system into orbit?

Brian

We call this the *law of three*. There are three legs to the stool of financial freedom, and they are *savings*, *insurance*, and *investment*. The best way is to go through them one at a time. First is savings. You need between two and six months of normal expenditures put aside, so that if you lost your job you'd be able to continue with your current standard of living for two to six months.

If you have that, you have tremendous confidence in dealing with your world. I've spoken with countless people to whom I've given this advice, and they went back and they darn well did it. It took them a year to get two months of savings put aside, they really were strict with themselves, and then they got a new boss, or their old boss became a tyrant, or the company began to increase their hours and reduce their pay, and they said, "Phooey!" and walked away. They could do it because they had money in the bank, whereas their coworkers had to stay there and take the new negative conditions.

I remember a woman who wrote to me about this. She had thought the purpose of her income was to go out and spend it on clothes, cosmetics, and having a good time, but when she heard my advice, she realized that she was trapped. If she didn't have a paycheck every month, she would be desperate. She literally stopped spending for a year and said it transformed her life, because now she had this money.

So the first one is you need two to six months income in savings. Six is best, but at least go for two before anything else.

The second thing you need to do is to insure properly. This is so important. An accountant friend of mine once said to insure against anything that you can't write a check for, so you get health insurance. I was talking recently to someone who had let his health insurance go. To save money for skiing, he had let his health insurance lapse, and then he broke his back while skiing. He was laid up for six months, and then recuperating for six more months of physical therapy. It set back his whole life, because he had let his health insurance expire.

You need automobile insurance, both collision and liability. You need complete home insurance. Again, if your home burned down, you couldn't write a check for it.

We went to an insurance agency, and said, "Here's our life, what do we need?" They're experienced. They said, "You need to be insured here, you don't need this much insurance there, you could do with this much insurance here, but you want some of that there." They walked us through, and they bought different policies from different agencies for different matters and so on, and we've never had a single financial problem.

And of course raising four children over thirty years, you have a lot of unexpected reversals, so it's really important to have the right insurance, simultaneous with accumulating two to six months' income. Be sure that you insure properly. Don't listen to these people that say insurance is gambling against yourself. You also need life insurance. If you're the primary breadwinner for your family, you need insurance to be able to take care of your family for the indefinite future if something should happen to you.

By the way, this gives you a tremendous psychological boost and great piece of mind. It also makes you stronger and more forceful, more positive in the rest of your life to know that your back and your family's back are completely covered. You are far more confident taking greater risks.

Dan

Brian, to wrap up this chapter, are there any other ideas or concepts on debt that we have not yet touched on?

Brian

Let me summarize our discussion about debt, because I have been deeply in debt and I know the psychological and emotional implications. Lying awake at night for fear of having your home repossessed, parking your car two blocks away so that it's not picked up by the repo people—this is an awful way to live, and yet many times you run near to this situation. If it happens, it happens, and if it's happened to you, just make a decision to get out of debt and stay out of debt for life. Your motto going forward is, "I'm going to live debt-free for life."

Then sit down and make a plan and move this to the top of your list of priorities. This isn't something you're going to do some-day; this is something you're going to do *now*. If you're married, sit down with your spouse and make a list of every single asset that you have, and of every expense you have on a monthly basis—rent, utilities, gasoline, food, everything—and then make a list of every debt and lay it all out on paper.

I have said that you become what you think about most of the time. Self-made millionaires are people like you, but who at one time decided, "I'm going to become wealthy," and then they did. You never become wealthy prior to making that decision. If you do make that decision and you back it up with action, it's almost impossible for you *not* to become financially independent, because there are so many ways to achieve it.

They found out how much time people who are suffering financial problems spend thinking about their money each month. They think about that twenty-four hours a day. They think about it, they talk about it, they whine about it, they cry about it, they fight about it, they argue about it, they drive along thinking about their financial problems all the time. But how much time do you spend actually sitting down, writing out, planning, and thinking about your financial destiny, making plans?

The answer is, about one hour a month. People tend to sit down about one hour a month. It's mostly bill paying time. I've been through this, where you sit down and say, "All right, how much are we going to pay on this credit card this month, how much are we going to pay on that bill this month?" You allocate the money until it's pretty much all gone, and you get back to worrying about money for the next month.

What do self-made millionaires do? They spend ten hours a month or more sitting down. They read financial magazines, they read financial publications, they check out financial newsletters, they look at financial debt consolidations and investments. They spend ten hours a month thinking about how to organize their financial lives better, so they have a 1000%—ten times—advantage over the average person who doesn't.

If you're really serious about getting out of debt, even if you're not a detail person, make it a habit to buy a book or magazine on money. Listen to programs on money—audio programs, radio programs, and online. There are some fabulous programs on how people got out of debt. Make this a top priority: that you are going to get out of debt and stay out of debt for the rest of your life. If you make that a decision and write it down as a goal and make a plan, and then really put some shoulder into thinking about it as much as possible, you'll be quite astonished at how you can transform the rest of your financial life.

FIVE

The Science of Generating Income

Once you are employing smart spending methods and effective debt management methods consistent with the principles of the Science of Money, you need to make sure that you are generating strong cash flow or income, both to invest in further projects and financial opportunities and also to begin living the lifestyle you desire.

In this chapter, Brian will teach you the proven laws and principles you need to follow to generate the highest income possible, whether you are an employee, a business owner, or a full-time investor.

Dan

Brian, let's begin by discussing your own life experience as it relates to generating income. In the past, you have shared the story of how you went from working very hard at low-paying jobs in your early days to earning millions of dollars a year in cash flow as an author and business owner. What are some of the lessons you learned about how to generate an income that helps you fund your dreams?

Brian

Everybody wants to generate a consistently high income that enables them to fund their dreams. Everybody dreams of having money that comes in the mailbox, as they say, so that they are earning money and they're not working for it. This is largely a fantasy.

I know some of the smartest people in the world who have had this fantasy for twenty-five years. They're always saying, "This is the one. This is going to be the trick. This is the way that I will start to generate high levels of income without working."

The fact of the matter is the only way that you can do this is by investing time and money, and producing products that sell, or that other people sell, and which generate royalties, a commission, a dividend, or something else. For example, when I started to work very hard to become successful, I started to invest in income producing real estate. This turned out to be the best investment I'd ever made, because real estate continues. It's solid. It continues to grow in value. Your rents and leases from real estate continue to grow up with inflation and cost of living increases and so on. You'll find that most of the great fortunes are founded, first of all, in a productive business, and then they channel that money into income producing real estate, or into other investments that produce cash flow.

Dan

What is the biggest misconception most people have about how to generate a high income?

Brian

To go back to what we've talked about earlier, your work is a commodity that people buy at the lowest possible price, for the highest possible quality.

In the last couple of years I've done an enormous amount of work in two areas. One is called *business model reinvention*, which is taking a look at your business model. The other is called *personal life model reinvention*, taking a look at your personal life model. Both models are revenue generation methodologies—how do you generate profits for a business; how do you generate income for yourself?

The answer is that 90% of your income is going to be determined by the quality of the work you do in comparison with that of others who do the same work. Ninety percent of your success in business will be the result of the quality of the product that you offer in comparison with your competitors, who are offering a similar product that will do a similar thing. The greatest focus always has to be on increasing the quality of your product or service as a company, and increasing the quality of your work as an individual.

I'll give you an example. A friend of mine, a very wealthy businessman, very successful, very conservative, needed to have open-heart surgery. He said, "Wow. Even though this is pretty standard today, people do die on the table from open-heart surgery."

He began to do some research to find the best surgeon in the country for his particular type of surgery. He found this surgeon at the Cleveland Clinic, which is world-famous for having the foremost heart surgery specialists in the world. He contacted him through his doctor, finally made arrangements, and then flew to

Cleveland for his surgery. He spent seven days in the hospital and came back on a private jet. He told me, "If you're going to have open-heart surgery, this is the guy. He's done this surgery more than 5000 times and has an absolutely impeccable success rate. If you're really going to need open-heart surgery and you want to be absolutely guaranteed that you recover and have a normal life afterwards, you have to go to this guy."

Of course this doctor is paid an absolute fortune. An open-heart surgeon in a normal city may get something like $50,000; he gets $250,000. Not only that, he does four a day. It takes about ninety-two minutes to two hours to do an open-heart surgery.

I know this because I subsequently had open-heart surgery with another doctor, also one of the best in the country, who also had done 5000 surgeries, and who also does between two and four surgeries a day. You only see him once beforehand. The next time you and he cross paths, you are unconscious. He does the surgery, and you never see him again. He's a genius, and he probably gets $150,000 to $250,000 per operation, two to four times a day, because he's in the absolute elite of his field.

I use this example to emphasize my belief that if you're going to invest money at all, invest money in becoming really excellent at what you do. I talk about this over and over again in my seminars. I'm not asking you to win the gold medal in the Olympics or be number one, just be in the top 10%, because that's where all the money is.

One reason people are not in the top 10% in their field is that they've chosen the wrong field completely and they have no capability for it. But the major reason is, they never decided to be in the top 10%, and they just coasted. They reached a certain level of competence, and then they coasted.

One of the most important studies on elite performance has been done by Dr. K. Anders Ericsson at the University of Florida. He's the one who says it takes 7000 to 10,000 hours of hard work and five to seven years to enter into the levels of elite performance.

He's done most of his work with musicians, but also in other fields as well. Malcolm Gladwell wrote his book *Outliers* citing the research that Ericsson had done. And then Geoffrey Colvin of *Fortune* wrote *Talent Is Overrated* based on exactly the same idea—that you don't have to have talent to start off with, but if you really put in the hours, you can develop yourself to the point where you perform at an extraordinary level.

As long as it's the right field for you, you love it, you enjoy it, you put your whole heart into it. You enjoy becoming better and better. You can't become excellent at something that you don't love, that your heart isn't in.

Anyway, Ericsson found that the average person, in the bottom 80%, will work to develop competence and confidence in their job, and then they will level off and never get any better. The average person—80% of the population—is no more productive ten years after they start their first job than they were after one year. It's only the top 20% of people who continue to grow.

Gary Becker, a Nobel Prize–winning economist, did an interesting study. He found that the average income of people in the bottom 80% goes up about 2% or 3% per year, as long as they remain employed. This is about the increase in the cost of living, so they never get ahead. For the people in the top 20%, their income goes up at an average of 11.8% per year, because they're continually learning, and growing, and increasing their skills, and getting better and better in their fields.

So why do some people earn high incomes? It's because they do their jobs very, very well.

I'll give you some great examples. Just think of the chefs who run the top restaurants, like Alain Ducasse, who runs a restaurant in New York. It's one of the most famous restaurants in the world. It's fully booked, and people easily pay $500 to $1000 a night for two people to go there and have dinner.

The top restaurant in the United States is called The French Laundry, and it's located in the Napa Valley, which is very hard to get to. You have to fly into Oakland or San Francisco. You have to drive an hour and a half to two hours. You have to stay at a hotel up there in the Napa Valley in order to go to this restaurant.

This restaurant has such high quality that the basic dinner is between $350 and $500, and wine is extra. You can only make a reservation one year out, and they take your credit card and full payment upon reservation.

You can't change your mind, or change your date, or have a no-show, so people literally travel from all over the world. They fly in. They stay at a nearby hotel, and they go to this restaurant, so that they can experience the gourmet cooking of the chef who runs The French Laundry. This is an extreme example of how if you're really, really good at what you do, people will pay you almost anything.

As we know, a lawyer gets $200 to $300 an hour. The best lawyers get $2000 or $3000 an hour, $10,000 an hour. Sometimes they get $100,000 or $200,000 or $1 million to handle a particular case, because if you can get this lawyer to take your case, whatever it happens to be, it can save you or make you a fortune.

When it comes to earning a high income, there's only one way to do it, and that's to be so good at what you do that a conscious consumer, wanting the very most for the very least, eagerly pays you premium dollars for your product or your service or your labor.

One last thing to keep in mind is that all fortunes in America start with the sale of personal services. A person becomes very, very good at delivering personal services. As a result people are willing to pay them premiums, and to hire them, and to promote them, and move them up, and give them greater responsibilities. And with greater responsibilities comes more money, and with more money becomes more opportunity, and so on. But it all loops back to doing what you do in a really excellent fashion.

Dan

Some employees will say they put a lot of time and effort into a company, and they should be paid more for that. Speaking as someone who employs people, how would you respond to them?

Brian

That's very common. People say, "I've got 20 years' experience," but the boss says, "Quite honestly, you've only got one year of experience twenty times over," because, remember, the great majority—80% or more—only do their jobs well enough to not get fired and to avoid the antagonism of their fellow workers because they're not doing their share. Once they reach that point, they slip into a comfort zone. They hang out. They chitchat. They go for lunch and coffee. They waste time.

This is one of the great tragedies. People go to work, and the first thing they do is go and find somebody to talk to, and then after they've spoken to that person, they go and find somebody else to talk to, and somebody else to talk to. They never start to work. They don't go in at 8:30 and start work. They go and find somebody to talk to, and then they go, "Geez, it's 11 o'clock, and I've talked to all my friends about what was on TV, and what movies they saw, and the family, and the latest news story," and so on.

Only then do, they go to work and, oh my gosh, it's lunchtime. They all go out for lunch, and then they come back after lunch, which is usually too long, and they reestablish their relationship with their friends, talk, talk, talk, and then do a little bit more work, and then they leave because they want to beat the traffic. And they wonder why they don't get promoted. We see this over and over again.

In our company, as I've said, if a person does a really good job, we give preemptive increases. We don't want to lose them, because good people are really rare. Good people are the hardest thing to get, and once you get them, pay them whatever they require to keep them, because a good person costs nothing. A good person contributes far more value than they cost.

As a matter of fact, the most successful companies are the ones that keep hiring people that contribute more, in either cost savings or revenue increases, than they cost. So each new person actually yields a net profit to the company. That's why companies who have 100,000 employees make hundreds of millions and billions of dollars a year, because every employee is actually contributing more than they cost.

This is really the key. When a person says "I want more money," the fact is that they're not earning more money. I had a guy come up to me recently at a talk where I was saying you should set a goal to double your income, and he came up to me at the break, very superior, arrogant, and said, "This might be a nice motivational talk that you're giving, but in my company there's no way they would pay me twice as much. So what you're saying is really not true, and you should make it clearer to the audience that it's a bit of an exaggeration."

I said, "OK, let me ask you a question. Is there anybody in your company that earns twice as much as you?" He stopped and said, "Well, yes, of course." "Are there people that earn three, or four, or five times as much as you?" "Well, yeah, the senior people, the top people."

"So then," I said, "we can safely conclude that your company is more than willing to pay people three or four or five times what you earn. They're just not willing to pay *you* that amount. Now why would that be?" He was shocked, as if I'd slapped him in the face. And he said, "Maybe it's because I'm not very productive." I said, "There you go. It's your fault. *You're* the reason why you're not getting paid more money." He walked away shaking his head.

I call it the survival bonus: "Boss, I didn't die last year, so therefore I'm entitled to more money." No, you're only entitled to more money if you're producing more value. Your share of the extra value you're creating constitutes your increase. No increase in value, no increase in pay.

Dan

One of the most frequent complaints around the water cooler at work is the fact that many people do not feel they are paid what they're worth. Many people feel that office politics, favoritism, etc., keep them from earning a salary commensurate with the value they are delivering. What do you recommend that an employee should do in this case?

Brian

It boils down to something for nothing—people think that they are entitled to more money, even though they don't do anything else to achieve it.

In the 1950s, something like 50% of the work force was unionized. This idea of unionization, which still exists in many government areas and with teachers, is that you get increased pay if you don't die. Therefore you have seniority. You're entitled to increased pay. People who have been there longer get paid more. Younger people get less money, even if they're hard-working and competent.

This filters down into a mind-set that you should be paid more based on the number of years that you've put in. This is the mind-set of people who want more money without earning it, who think they should get more money without being more productive, without creating more value. The fact of the matter is that in every company where people are being paid extremely well, even though they may have started after you, they are contributing more and more value.

And so the question is always, are you contributing more value now than last week, last month, last year? Are you getting more results that people value and will pay for? Are you contributing more value that, combined with the work of others, your company can use to sell more products and services, generate more sales, and more profitability? If you're not, then you haven't earned an automatic increase.

The days of the automatic increase have been gone for almost twenty years, and there are still people standing around the water cooler, wasting time, chatting with their friends, putting in their hours, and complaining that they're not getting paid more.

So if you want to get paid more, it's very simple. Start a little earlier. Work a little harder. Stay a little later. One thing I teach is that the key to success is to work all the time you work. It's always been the key to success. It's been the truth throughout history, especially in the last 200 years. When you go to work, work. Put your head down and work.

Sometimes I'll ask this question. Let's say you've got a job at McDonald's, a minimum wage job shaking French fries. Many people start their working careers with a job at McDonald's because it teaches them to work, to come on time, to cooperate, to follow instructions, to do good work, to clean up after themselves, and so on. This is very good training. So you get a job at McDonald's. Could you stroll into McDonald's fifteen or twenty minutes after your shift starts, holding a cup of Starbucks with your phone in your hand, checking on Facebook, and then hunker down with your friends and shoot the breeze about what you did last night and what you watched on TV, and then take half an hour for coffee and an hour for lunch, and so on?

Could you do that if you were working at McDonald's, at minimum wage? Absolutely not. You'd have to be there on time, punched in. If you're not punched in, you lose your job. Then you work, and you get a ten-minute coffee break in the morning, ten minutes in the afternoon, and thirty minutes at lunch, and you work your whole shift from eight to five.

Everybody knows that; that's what you have to do at a minimum wage job. So how much more important is it if you're a much higher-paid person, working in a white-collar environment? You're getting paid several times the minimum wage, ideally. How is it you think that you can go to work carrying your cup of Starbucks, and showing up late, and shooting the breeze, and hanging out and reading the paper and checking your e-mail, and not doing any work?

The whole audience has this shocked look, because they see themselves. They say, "I couldn't get away with that if I was working at McDonald's, and yet I'm trying to get away with it at work, and I'm wondering why I never get my work done. I'm wondering why I'm behind the eight ball. I'm wondering why I haven't had an increase for three years. I'm wondering why I'm not making any progress in my career." It's because you're not working.

Dan

You're absolutely right. I could never imagine *not* being fired for showing up fifteen minutes late every day for your McDonald's job. That's so true, but we often think of it so differently with a white-collar job.

Now let's discuss the science of generating income for business owners. This is a huge issue, since many businesses never get off the ground, or survive past a couple of years because of low cash flow.

First, what should the expectations be for a new business owner for generating income in the first year or two? Do you recommend that a potential entrepreneur only proceed if he or she has a year or two of income in the bank? Why or why not?

Brian

There are two questions with regard to cash flow and money in the bank. Everything comes down to sales. IBM got into serious economic trouble between '89 and '91. The stock price dropped 80%. They were talking about breaking up the company.

It was a major deal, because in the '80s IBM was the most respected company in the world. High profits, great leadership, fabulous technology, greatest customer service, ranting raves in all the magazines—*Fortune, Forbes, Business Week.* Two or three years later it fell out of the sky.

So they fired the president and brought in a new president, Lou Gerstner, who knew nothing about computers. He said, "I don't even know how to turn one on, but I do know about business." He'd started off his career working for McKinsey & Company, one of the best and largest management consulting companies in the world. If they accept the assignment, they come in and fan out. They find the problem, and the solution to the problem. They always come in with a solution that works, which is why they're paid so much.

After six months and about $3 million worth of consulting fees, they sat down the senior people at IBM and said, "We found your problem. It's low sales." They all rolled their eyes and said, "We know that. That's why our stock price is down—low sales, low profits."

They asked what the solution was. The consultants said, "High sales." And it's interesting, because Dun & Bradstreet studied the autopsies of tens of thousands of companies that have gone broke over the years, and found that you could put aside all the other explanations—technological, capitalization, competition—it all came down to low sales. IBM asked McKinsey & Company what the solution was. The solution was very simple, they said. "We've looked at the time usage of your salespeople and sales managers, and we found that under the previous administration they've been reduced almost to performing as accountants," because the previous administrators had been accountants, and they always believe that accounting is the most important function in a business.

Instead of going out and making calls, salespeople were expected to spend 75% of their time filling out forms. If they did make a call, they'd have to fill out a five-page sales form. Then the sales managers had to spend all their time reviewing the forms filled out by the salespeople, and nobody was talking to customers.

The consultants said, "Our recommendation is to flip it upside down. People are going to spend less than 25% of their time in the office and 75% of their time face-to-face with customers. Sales managers are going to spend 75% of their time with their salespeople talking to customers." So they began the 75% rule.

They got them out there talking to customers, and the whole company turned around. It went from $1.5 billion in losses to $1.6 billion in profits in one year. The stock went up. Today it's still one of the best-performing stocks in the world.

This rule is now used all over the world in major corporations, because the magic of the turnaround at IBM was reported widely. Very simply, get your salespeople and your sales managers to spend 75% of their time doing sales. If you are a small business, get the owner of the business out there with customers 75% of the time.

The point is that it is always low sales that lead to business problems, and it is always high sales that lead to business success.

Concerning how much should you have put aside, how much should you have as reserves, and how much should you take: the answer is, how much can you sell? They did a study of small to medium-sized business owners recently, and the analysts asked how important marketing and sales, and new customer generation, were to their businesses.

They all said, "Oh, the most important thing of all; there's nothing more important than sales and marketing. It's the blood to the brain. It's oxygen. We die without it." "How much of your time do you, as the company owner, the chief decisionmaker, spend on sales and marketing?" "All the time, all day. It's all I ever think about, morning, noon, and night."

The analysts then asked, "Could we come in with time and motion specialists and just walk around, with a note pad and stopwatch, and watch how you use your time on a day-to-day, week-to-week basis?" "Oh, absolutely, no problem at all."

So they analysts went in, and after a month they came back with their results: the average business owner spends 11% of his or her time in sales and marketing. Everything else is checking on e-mail, social media, chatting with staff, going for lunch, meeting with the banker, and so on.

That's why they were struggling. If you spend 11% of your time on sales, the staff will probably spend less than that, because you always set the standard in your company, and everybody follows you.

I've given this advice over and over again. People come back, and they're absolutely shocked. Their business, which had been struggling, suddenly transforms into a high-sales, high-profit business, because people are out there selling the product all day long. I said, "When did you do your paperwork, before 8 o'clock and after 6 o'clock?" The rule is, you do not do administrative work when there are customers to be seen. When there are customers to be seen, all you do is see customers.

I had a business owner who came to me for one full day of strategy, and we talked about the best use of his time. He considered the best use of his time to be search engine optimization, so that's what he was working on. I asked, "Are you a technical person?" He said, "No, I'm not a technical person, but it's the key to generating new business for our companies to generate more online leads."

"This may be an important activity," I said, "but it's *not your* important activity. What are the things that you do that generate the most new revenues? What are the activities, specifically?" We went back and forth and looked over all his activities, and he realized that most of his best new business came from recommendations and referrals from his top 20% of clients.

"Then," I said, "the best use of your time would be to spend more time face-to-face, or phone-to-phone, with your very best clients, making sure that they're happy, offering them additional services, giving them coaching, consulting advice, information." He said, "You're absolutely right. It's so obvious. The more time I spend with my best clients, the more they buy of my services, and the more they bring in their friends who are at the same level that they are. This is going to transform my business." He went back, and he had me come in and teach this entire process to everybody in his company.

They went from $10 million to $20 million in sales in 2008–2009, when the market was tanking. They transformed the business. Their sales went up, and their profits went up even faster, by focusing on customers, focusing on making sales.

What is the main reason companies fail? One is that they do not aggressively sell the product. There's always an excuse, or they try to run ads, online ads, when there are 36 million people running online ads to sell stuff. They think, "I'll just put some ads on the Internet, and then I'll make a lot of money." No, in most cases, you're going to have to make direct personal contact.

People don't buy products and services. They buy the people, the individuals who sell them, and they buy them because they like them and trust them more than they like other people who offer similar products or services, so you have to be really focused on this.

The second reason companies fail is that nobody wants the product. *Forbes* just completed a study and found that 80–90% of business failure occurs because nobody wants the product in the first place. The people selling the product think it's a good product. They even think that other people should buy it. In many cases they themselves don't use it, and nobody in their company uses it, but they think it's good for other people.

I was quite astonished in working with a very successful company that sold motivational audio programs, with some with the best motivational speakers, with the best ideas and information. I went throughout the entire company and found that nobody in the company listens to the products.

They think these products are good for others, but they never touch them. They never listen to them. They never have them in their cars. They drive around listening to music or talk radio. They never listen to the products that they sell, and, surprise, surprise, companies like that eventually go out of business, because, as they say, you have to drink your own Kool-Aid.

I often ask, how many of the people in your company use your product exclusively? It's astonishing—as many as 50–70% of people in the company use the competitors' products. They don't use the product that they sell, and as a result, when they do offer it, they have no heart. If you use something yourself and you think it's fabulous, you can talk about it with conviction and enthusiasm, but if you don't, then you can't.

So the main problem is poor sales, and the second is that people just don't want the product or service, and they'll tell you that quite quickly.

In economics we say that every customer has three choices. They can buy your product. They can buy your competitor's product. Or they can buy nothing at all. That's what you have to deal with with every customer contact.

Dan

Does the research show a particular percentage that an owner should take from the business as a salary? What should entrepreneurs expect to take as income?

Brian

There is no exact answer for that. It depends upon the success of the business. If you're generating high levels of profitability, you can take more income; if you're not, you can't take any.

When I was starting my business, I didn't take any income from it for two years. All I did was generate enough income to keep it alive, and as I told you earlier, I had to sell my house and my car, and borrow from everybody that I knew. And then I moved my business from Canada to the U.S. and started it again, and eventually staffed it up to twenty people.

Again, I wasn't able to take any income out of my business for about two years. I had to take income from every other source: royalties, and books, and audio programs, and everything else. I even had to borrow to keep the business running, until finally it started to yield profits.

I had to put an enormous amount of money into product development, and product development costs are all up-front. Product *sales* are iffy; maybe they happen in the end. But you have to pay 100% for product development, for stocking up your company, before you even get a chance to sell it—unless you do something like what we talked about earlier, where you represent other products. Then you don't have to buy them until you've sold them, so you basically take the money in between.

It's very common that you don't take any money out of your business. You basically scramble for the first couple of years. But let me tell you another interesting point. *Inc.* magazine does a study of the 500 fastest-growing companies every year, and in the latest review, they looked at the founders of these companies.

The fastest-growing company of all in the latest study had grown 4200 times in three years. That's 42,000%. Many of the companies had grown fifty or 100 times, which is phenomenal. Most companies would be happy if they grew 10% or 20%.

They found two things in common among the founders of these companies that really grew. Number one is they started the company because they loved the product, and really got excited about it for themselves and their families. Only secondarily did they find that other people loved it as well.

The company that grew 42,000% had developed an early education program for children in primary schools, tied into an iPad, where they could help their kids get straight A's, and it was a really great concept. And every other parent in America said, "I want that. I want my kid to get started off in first, second, third grade with straight A's. That sets him up for life. They have an expectation for life of getting straight A's." Parents began to storm the company asking for it. The company grew 42,000%, and they started it because they wanted to help their kids.

Another entrepreneur, Hamdi Ulukaya, started Chobani yogurt, because he came from Turkey and he really liked Greek yogurt. It was very high in protein, very high-quality, and they didn't offer it anywhere here. We had this wimpy, milky, watered-down yogurt. Hamdi started to manufacture Greek yogurt at home and sold it to local stores. It started to sell like hotcakes, even though it cost twice as much as normal yogurt. His story is phenomenal. He ended up buying a bankrupt yogurt factory in upstate New York, borrowing the money, borrowing the facilities, manufacturing Chobani on a large scale. It's now one of the fastest- and biggest-selling yogurts in North America. My family would never use anything but Chobani, even though it costs twice as much, because it's so excellent. And remember, he started it because he liked the flavor of Greek yogurt.

So when people say, "I want to start a business," I say, "Make sure that you're going to offer a product or service that you want for yourself, that you want for your family, that you'd sell to your mother, and to your father, and to your best friends because you think it is so good that it would really make a difference in their lives."

That's the starting point. That doesn't mean that you'll be successful, but without that, chances are, based on the research, you'll never put your whole heart into the business. You'll be playing golf on Fridays, and taking time off, and shooting the breeze, living off whatever you can beg, borrow, and steal until the company goes broke.

Those are the two main reasons companies go broke in the first couple of years: because the product is not wanted, or because they don't vigorously sell it.

Dan

Brian, what is the shift in mind-set that someone has to go through as they earn money and plan the cash flow of a business, as opposed to getting a steady paycheck every two weeks?

Brian

Experts have studied times of major layoffs, when thousands of people get laid off—industry downturns like those in aerospace or technology or other shifts in the economy. Many times people get laid off with a big lump of severance pay, sometimes several hundred thousand dollars. They've been working for ten or twenty years. They've built up their reserves, and they're paid on them.

So then these people decide, "Well, doggone it, I'm going to start my own business," which is becoming more and more common. The biggest group, percentagewise, of new business startups is people in their fifties, surprisingly enough, and an even bigger percentage is women. Women are starting businesses more often than men—of all ages.

The first thing that happens to these new business owners is that they are shocked that they have to do everything themselves—little things like answering the phone, emptying the wastebaskets, making the coffee, packing boxes, and so on. If they've worked for a large or even medium-sized company, it has a division of labor. When people start their own businesses, there's nobody else there. Earl Nightingale used to say that the biggest mistake you could ever make is to think that you work for anybody else but yourself. It's only once your business starts to become successful that you can afford to get help.

When I started my business, I had no illusions at all. I got a typewriter, and I typed my own sales letters, and my own letters of agreement with clients. I had to do my own mailing. To get something professionally typed, I'd have to take it to a typist. To get something produced, I'd have to design it, take it to a designer, take it to a printer.

I had been working for a year, flat-out hard work. I designed my own brochures. I made my own sales calls. I brought people into my own seminars. I wrote up the name tags. I delivered the seminar. I served the coffee. I set up the tables and chairs.

I did 100% of it myself, with my wife helping me. It was only after a year, a year and a half, that I got one-third of a secretary, because I worked with two other guys who were consultant salespeople. We had one secretary, Monica, and we had one-third each. It was only after another six months that my business had grown enough that I was able to hire Monica full-time. So I had my first full-time employee who could do all the little things that I had been doing, and then a second, and then a third, and so on.

But that's how it works when you start a business. We've said before that if you start a business with too much money, and you start hiring too many people, it's astonishing how fast you can go through all your cash. Therefore the first thing you have to understand is that you're going to be responsible for everything, especially revenue generation.

I've seen so many business owners lose everything. They say, "I will hire a good salesperson." No, you won't, because good salespeople won't work for you. That's because they're already selling something and making really good money at it, with an established company, an established product line, an established clientele, and a reputation in the marketplace.

I remember that I made this mistake. I hired this salesman. His name was Dennis, and he was absolutely awful. He had a great story about what a top salesperson he was, but basically he bled my company dry, promising me roomfuls of customers, piles of sales, checks coming in any minute. I don't think he ever made a sale in three months.

He took a big draw, and took commissions on sales that he was supposed to have made. After three months, I confronted him, and he walked out, and I never saw him again. And so I learned that I had to make all the sales myself.

I'm really big on the importance of the sales function. If you're not a salesperson, you find a partner who is. One of the great partnerships was Hewlett-Packard. Bill Hewlett was tremendous at engineering and developed the first product for Hewlett-Packard, which was an oscilloscope. Dave Packard was a fabulous marketer and salesman.

This turned out to be one of the great partnerships in world business history. Bill and his ever-growing squad of engineers developed fabulous products. Dave and his ever-growing squad of marketing and salespeople went out and sold them all over the world.

So if you're the kind of person who has no sales ability, and if you're not paired with someone who is really good at selling, don't start a business. It's just too dangerous.

Dan

Finally, for investors, what are some of the best strategies you know for generating a strong and consistent income from your investments, be they financial investments, like stocks, bonds, and annuities, or real estate investments?

Brian

The most important thing to realize is that when you buy an investment, you are gambling against the knowledge and experience of the person who is selling it. You are believing that it will go up in value. They are believing that it won't, or, even worse, that it will go down. That's why every stock exchange is a zero-sum game. The person selling it believes that it's maxed out in value. The person buying it hopes that it's going to go higher.

With regard to real estate, income-producing real estate, commercial real estate, is one of the best foundations for a fortune. But commercial real estate is not a slam dunk.

I have two friends who are full-time experts in commercial real estate, with ten, twenty years of experience. They developed, owned, and operated millions of dollars' worth of commercial real estate office buildings, industrial buildings, hotels, and so on. They both went bankrupt when the market went down, because they had mortgages. The mortgages were based on the leases, but the clients went bankrupt because the economy went down. They did not have enough money to carry the building. The buildings were taken back by the banks and the mortgage companies, and they both ended up bankrupt. They had to sell their homes, everything. They moved into rented premises with their families, and they had to, basically, go back on the street earning a living, and they had been multimillionaires.

So you should know there are people who go bankrupt in commercial real estate all the time. You know that 30% of shopping centers in America today are bankrupt, or nearly bankrupt, because it's so much easier to buy millions of items online. You don't have to get in the car, drive across town, find a parking space, go to a store, find that they don't have your size, or your color, or what you were looking for. You can just go online, click, click, you can get the exact size, shape, color, at a discount price delivered to your door the next day.

Now 30% of shopping centers are going bust and being converted into bowling alleys and gyms, or public service operations, where, instead of shelves and products in stores, they have desks.

The very best investment is something that yields you a steady, consistent, positive cash flow. In some investments that I've gone into, they will actually sell you a piece of property yielding no cash flow. You'll buy it at breakeven. It earns you nothing. You pay for the money. You have to pay for the mortgage. You have to give personal guarantees and all you do is break even, because the property is earning just enough to pay the mortgage.

Why? It's because the following year you can raise the rents a little bit, and the following year you can raise the rents a little bit more, like the example I gave you with the apartment. I actually bought a property where it was costing me money to service it each month, but I had a tenant, and then I just increased the rents gradually.

So, today, I've gone into multimillion-dollar investments where you just break even, but it's a good project, and the project is in a growing area, and the project is solid. If you just hang in there, after the first or second year, you're making a slight profit the third or fourth year. Sometimes it takes about seven years before you're actually making a positive cash flow that pays back the dry years. This is very, very common in buying commercial property.

Dan

Brian, give us the key takeaways of the principles of income and taking income as an investor or an employee.

Brian

First of all, generating income is always risky, because everybody wants income. Everybody wants high income. Everybody wants assured income. As a good friend of mine said speaking to an MBA class, the three factors that you're going to have to deal with throughout your career, which are going to determine everything that happens to you, are competition, competition, and competition.

Everybody wants the good life. Everybody wants to earn good money. Everybody wants a steady cash flow. Everybody wants profits and a good standard of living. So in everything that you do, you are surrounded by hundreds of thousands, millions, of people who are competing with you to get the same limited amount of cash flow.

That is why, as Warren Buffett says, the best investment you can make is into index funds. I mentioned that Buffett spends 80% of his time studying his investments. Carlos Slim, one of the richest men in the world, spends 80% of his time studying his investments. That's who you're going against. You're going against brilliant people with decades of experience, who have incredible amounts of knowledge, and access to the smartest people in the world, and even they make mistakes 25–30% of the time.

Therefore the best thing of all, if you're going to invest, is to invest with experts, people with proven track records, people with a history of making money, and also people who have their own money on the line along with yours. The best investments I ever made were with people who would put their money in next to mine, and who made nothing unless I made money. We made money at exactly the same rate and exactly the same percentage. Those are the best investments of all.

SIX

The Science of Creating Wealth

Earlier in "The Myths about Money," we discussed how most wealthy people don't focus on the acquisition of money; they focus on creating wealth. This is a major distinction, because in treating money as a scientific discipline, we naturally would assume that money is a thing to be acquired, but in reality it is a means of exchange of value, a by-product of productive activity. In this chapter, Brian will clarify this difference. He will discuss how entrepreneurs, inventors, authors, and other creative professionals become some of the highest-paid people on the planet through creativity and innovation.

Dan

In this session we move to a higher level of the Science of Money. We might call this the graduate level. The earlier sessions dealt with ideas that, if employed, can lead to a financially secure and potentially financially free life. But if one desires great wealth, what the press refers to as the top 1%, then you have to think bigger by either adding value or creating new value. Talk about the difference between the *competitive mind-set*, where you compete against others to achieve success, versus the *creative mind-set*, where you add value and create a whole new category. Also explain why the latter pays so much better and is ultimately so much more secure.

Brian

Both the competitive and the creative mind-sets are very important. As I said before, we live in a highly creative world, where everybody wants to have a better standard of living. This explains everything that's happening with regard to the U.S. and Canada on the one hand, and China, Taiwan, Vietnam, and Indonesia on the other—the countries that are producing products at a much lower cost than we are. It's because they are acting on behalf of the customers of America who want to pay the very least for the very most.

IBM used to be the world giant in personal computers. They set a goal to have 50% of the market in five years; they had it in two years. Today IBM has sold 100% of its computer business to Lenovo in China, and China manufactures all IBM PCs, plus PCs for half the rest of the world, because they can make high-quality PCs at a much lower price than we can. Competition, competition, competition—it never stops.

Some people do get into the top 1%, or the top 0.01%, or 0.001%, but the odds are extraordinary—ninety-nine to one—so they require an enormous number of factors to come together simultaneously. Most people get rich slowly, and they get rich starting off with a single product. I've studied this for years. You start off with a single product, and you make that product successful. There's a series of stages that you're going to need to go through.

Let us say you want to start a business, and you want to be financially successful, and ultimately you want to be wealthy so that you can retire. That's very good and very healthy and eminently achievable. The first thing you do is you say, what would be my product? You define your product in terms of your *value offering*. The value offering is, what difference would this product make in the lives of my customer?

The two critical factors for business success, according to Jim Collins in his book *Good to Great*, are, first of all, you must have a product or service that matters. It must make a difference, it must mean something, it must be something that people want and need and care about. If you have a product that doesn't matter, the only way you can sell it is on the basis of clever advertising and reduced prices. But if you have something that's really important to people, you can charge more, and people will pay more.

The second factor is, it must be different and superior. It must be so clear that people will prefer to choose that of all the similar products that are available. A perfect example is the Apple iPhone. When the Apple iPhone came out, the world leaders were Blackberry, which had 49% of the world business market, and Nokia, which had 49% of the world's cell phone market overall. They both dismissed the iPhone as a toy.

But Apple realized that if you could combine all the different things that people wanted to be able to do—send pictures, send messages, download messages, check out restaurants, use applications and so on, combine them all in one place, plus take photographs and record music—you could create something that nobody else had ever done before. The giants of the industry, Blackberry and Nokia, dismissed it as a toy, said it was only for teenagers, and nobody was really going to want it; there would always be a market for a good, stable, old handset. Five years later they were bankrupt.

I ask my audiences this question: "Let's talk about something that matters. Have you ever gotten in your car and driven a few blocks or halfway to work and realized you left your phone at home?" And I'll ask 1000 people this; they'll nod. I'll say, "What did you do?" Everybody says, "Turned around and went back." That's something that matters. That is something that's so important that if you realize that you're without it, you'll go back and get it.

You have to have a product that matters, a product that makes a difference in people's lives. The value offering always says, what job does your product do that people are willing to pay your product to do for them? What problem does your product solve that is so pressing that people will pay you money? What benefit does your product give that is so important that people will sacrifice in order to own it? What goal does it help them to achieve? What pain does it take away? It's amazing how many products and services are bland. They don't answer these questions, and as a result they always fail.

Once you have your product idea, the second thing is, you have to test it. Today we're finding the best test is a customer test. You ask, who would be the ideal person for my product idea? Who would buy it the earliest and pay the most for it? Then you go to one or more of these customers and you talk to them personally. This is the revolution that's taking place in marketing today.

In the old days, companies would put together a new product and then announce it like a surprise, like the debut of a movie hitting the screens for the first time. Today more and more companies go to a potential customer and say, "I think this product would be perfect for you to help you improve the quality of your life or work. What do you think?" Your customers will give you feedback, and they'll say, "I like this, but I don't like that, and I like this, but I don't like that, and if you offered more of this or less of that . . ." Then you go back and adjust the product.

It's very similar to coming up with a new recipe. You have your family taste the recipe and ask, "What do you think of this?" "It's too salty or it's too hot or it's too sweet or it's too something." You go back, and you tinker with the recipe until everybody says it's really great. Now you know you've got it.

That's what's happening today in marketing. It's called *customer cocreation*. When you come up with a product idea and ask how this product can improve the life or work of your customer, you go to potential customers and you work with them hand in hand, until the customer absolutely agrees: "Yes, this is a great product, and I will pay you money now to be able to get it when you have it complete." The only thing that really matters is a financial transaction: personal acts that give you money. It's not only that they say it's good, but they actually will give you money so that they are first in line.

Think of the Apple releases, where people line up in the streets three days in advance and sleep there, with other people bringing them food and taking their place so they can go to the bathroom. I talk to business people and ask, "How many people do that when you come out with a new product?" And they just laugh. They say, "None, zero, ever."

So first you test the product to make sure that there's a market for it. Then you offer it in limited release and find out how much you can charge for it. And then you start to roll it out, and you develop a business model that enables you to get the most of your product or service to the greatest number of customers at the best price in the shortest period of time. Then you simply multiply that process and do it over and over again.

That's basically how people start a successful business. If you are lucky, you're going to come up with a product or a service that is revolutionary, but it's only then that you're going to move into the higher levels where you make an enormous amount of money. Bill Gates's Microsoft software was revolutionary. It became the de facto software for computers worldwide.

Here's an interesting point. Bill Gates did not create the software. He actually bought Microsoft software from someone else who had developed it, and then improved it dramatically. He decided to throw his software open to all developers in the world so that anybody could use the code and develop software built on the Microsoft platform. Steve Jobs and Bill Gates both started at the same time, in the early 1980s, and Steve Jobs decided to keep the maximum amount of profits possible by closing off the architecture and making it proprietary.

Within ten years, Bill Gates had 90% of the market, and Apple was down to 2%, even though many people said that Apple's was a superior computer, easier to use, more user-friendly, more beautiful, and everything else. But they had the wrong business model. When they brought out the iPhone in 2006, again they said, "We're going to develop the apps." So Apple developed a few apps, but they were finally convinced that they should open up the architecture and let other people develop them. They admitted that they just didn't have the resources to develop a large number of apps. Steve Jobs fought against this for a long time. Finally he agreed to open the architecture to app developers.

That was one of the greatest business decisions in history. It generated hundreds of millions and billions of dollars. It made Apple the richest company in the world, made their share value unbelievable. They have $200 billion in the bank right now after tax money. Everything hinged on that one twitch in the business model: open the architecture. Bill Gates was already the richest man in the world, because he had opened the architecture right at the beginning.

Sometimes you'll take a product or a service and combine it with a unique or different way of marketing that will transform the business. Ray Kroc came up with this idea when he saw the McDonald brothers and their hamburger stand in San Bernardino. He sold milkshake makers, and this company kept buying more and more milkshake makers. So he went down to see them, and he was quite amazed. They had a production line producing really high-quality hamburgers, French fries, and malts.

He said, "This is a great idea. They have taken this traditional hamburger joint thing, and they've turned it into a machine." People were lined up. Cars were coming from everywhere, and they were making a fortune. He went to the brothers and said, "Do you want to go into business with me?" They said, "Sure." "So we'll start a business, we'll share the ownership"—I think it was 50-50—"and I'll take your entire system back to my head office in Des Plaines, Illinois, and I'll duplicate it."

Kroc wanted to expand, and he went back to the McDonald brothers. He said he wanted to expand, but he had to borrow money and he'd have to take out mortgages. They said, no, no, no—they didn't want to do any of that. They were just a couple of nice guys in San Bernardino, a farming community; He said, "Then let me buy you out, buy out the name and the concept." They sold it to him for peanuts. The rest is history. The company became successful, and Ray Kroc became one of the richest people.

Here's another interesting point. People say they want to franchise their deals. I hear this a lot from entrepreneurs. It takes approximately seven or eight years to sell the first franchise operation. It takes seven or eight years to get your business so standardized that it is a guaranteed money machine, that it works like a Swiss watch, so you can open the doors and it just pumps out profits all day.

Then to prove that you have a system, you simply start another one and you duplicate it, almost like an amoeba, or cloning. You clone and you create a second one, and you install all the same systems—you make them identical, you don't deviate—to see if this also becomes a money machine. If they become identical money machines, you know you have something. Then you do a third year, because it takes seven years—we talked about this, the seven-year cycle—before you get all the bugs out of the system. Only then can you duplicate.

When Bill Gates got into trouble with Microsoft, he was licensing the software for IBM PCs to IBM. But then Microsoft got into financial troubles, as happens in recessions. Gates went to IBM and said, "Look, rather than you paying me a royalty each time you install Microsoft on a PC, why don't you just pay me $350,000 and I'll sell it to you?" They said, "No, we're not in the business of owning software, thank you so much, but we have no interest in buying Microsoft for $350,000." Can you imagine that?

So he had to make the company work, and he did. Today Microsoft could buy and sell IBM before breakfast without even making a blip on their financial statements. I always wonder what great genius at IBM made that decision. But this was a fluke. Now we look at Bill Gates and say, "Wow, the richest man in the world!" He almost wasn't. Ray Kroc gambled everything too.

Peter Drucker said, "Wherever you see a successful business, somebody once took a big chance and won." Self-made billion-aires are people who started with nothing and have made a billion dollars in their lifetime. They say that the first quality is hard work and self-discipline. The second quality is continuous learning, which we see with Warren Buffett. The third quality is willingness to take a risk: at a certain point they were willing to go all in, like Texas holdem, and push all their chips in for one card. They were willing to do that, and the right card came up. That's how you get into the top 0.001%. There is no story of anybody who didn't go all in but still became a billionaire. Of the many people who did go all in, the great majority lost everything, and had to start over again.

We talk about the top 1% versus 99%. They all start off the same, with the same natural abilities—no earning ability, no money, maybe a good or bad education or maybe not, and so on. How did these particular people get into the top 1%?

I found that it's not the top 1%, it's the top 3%. It's the top 3% who have clear, specific, written goals and plans that they work on, just as an architect designs an absolutely beautiful building and continually refines the blueprints. They work on written goals and plans, and these are the top 3%.

As you know from the studies, these people earn ten times as much as the average, they acquire ten times as much, they have much better lives, because they have written goals and plans. So it's not the 1% versus the 99%. It's the 3% versus the 97%.

They studied this at the American Management Association. They found that the successful people are not smarter, they don't have higher IQs, they didn't graduate with better grades, they didn't go to better colleges. They just did certain things differently, and one was that they had written goals and plans. When they started their own businesses, they wrote out very clear business plans, then step by step they created checklists to find products or services that would work for them.

I worked with some really good guys who decided to get into an MLM (multilevel marketing) business. They spent eighteen months going around the country, and looked at all the MLM businesses, of which there are hundreds, tried the products of all of them, and they finally found one that they really liked. This one was just perfect for them. It was ideal in terms of their interests, they liked the product, and so they signed on. They joined this MLM business. They had gone broke in a business before that hadn't worked out. They started again, and this time they became multimillionaires, because they did their homework.

The first time they went into the business, they had just run in pell-mell like dogs chasing cars. This time they sat down and they wrote goals. They said, "What did we learn from the last business? What kind of a product can we sell with pride? What kind of product that people will buy and buy over and over again?" They went through this carefully, and then they took a look at every product available with their checklist until they finally found one. Then they experimented with it on a small scale, and then they became huge successes. I know: I spoke with them and worked with them.

To become really wealthy is very rare, but you can dramatically increase the odds in your favor by doing careful planning in advance and thinking it through. As they say, don't lose money. Think it through carefully, and invest your time and your effort to study every detail of the business before you put your money in and make an irrevocable commitment.

Dan

The most common way people do this is as what Michael Gerber calls a *system entrepreneur.* This is someone who focuses on working on the system so that it can replicate and create greater value, as opposed to an entrepreneur, who just works on his or her craft in his or her small business. Discuss the difference between these two kinds of entrepreneurs.

Brian

First of all, very few business products are franchisable. The product has to be consumable. It has to be something that people buy over and over. It has to have something superior about it compared to all the other, similar products. There have to be a whole lot of things going on.

Second, to make a business successful for the first time, as we said, takes seven years, and you have to work in that business and put your whole heart into the business. The people who came up with this idea of work *on* the business rather than *in* the business had never built a successful business in their lives and still have not. Nobody that ever took advice from them has ever built a successful business either.

I had a good friend who fell in love with the idea of working *on* the business rather than *in* the business. He said, "I followed that advice hook, line, and sinker," he said, "until I was broke. Then I went back to working *in* the business."

I have a good friend who teaches business management. I was talking to him, and he said every successful business owner works in the business. There are no exceptions. He said, "Look at Bill Gates, perhaps the most successful single business owner in the history of man. He works in his business as chief architect officer all the time. He is in there with both hands. He has passed on the day-to-day management, the supervision, to the CEO, COO, but he's in his business all the time and always has been. From the time he was twelve years old he has been working intimately with both hands in the business."

I had a management consultant friend who had studied business for over twelve years. He studied hundreds of businesses, trying to look at the one quality that made businesses successful, and his opinion was, it was hands-on management. He wrote a book on it. These owners do their rounds, like a doctor checking the patient in the hospital. They take the pulse, they look at the eyes, the mouth, the face, the blood pressure. The doctor's got his hands on the patient the whole time.

Starting the business is very much like an emergency situation. If you go to an emergency room, you'll find the doctors and nurses are right there. They've got their hands on the patients all the time, because this is the critical moment.

I was reading something on the wall of a hospital some time ago, which said that with stroke, the first thirty minutes determine whether or not this person will live or walk or think or anything else; you've got to move fast. Here are the symptoms of a stroke, here's what to do immediately; here's where to go. It's like starting a business. When you start a business, it's red alert time. Every day is an exciting day, because it can make or break your business. An accumulation of bad days with no money coming in, no profits, no sales, and you go underwater.

You have to have your hands on the business to make it successful. Anybody who says that you don't is a person who has never had a successful business. As you know from your own experience, if you want to be successful, you've got to put your whole heart into it. You can increase the odds that you will be successful, but you can never guarantee them.

Dan

When we talk about creating wealth, we are talking about a different mind-set than the mind-set we hear about in the media. The media assume that there is a fixed pie of resources for which we all compete. We might call this the *scarcity mentality*, whereas the Science of Money teaches us that money is not divided, but rather created. We might call this the *abundance mentality*. Talk about the difference between these two different types of mentality.

Brian

It's a great question. For all of human history, the only way that wealth was usually transferred was through plunder. People owned estates they had taken by plunder, the dukes and barons and earls and kings and so on. The villagers were required to pay a tribute in the forms of 10% or 20% of their crops to the people who owned the land. They then took those crops and sold them. That was their major source of revenue. That's where we get our taxation today. It comes from the work of the people toiling on the land.

The barons would live in these fabulous castles and have fabulous lives. They would march out with jewels beyond belief when the average person was eating dirt and having to pay 10% or 20% of their earnings. This is what led to Robin Hood and all the other, similar myths of Europe. As we mentioned earlier, virtually all war is plunder. It's robbing and plundering and looting and taking everything you possibly can.

Ayn Rand talks about the development of capitalism in the late seventeenth century, the early 1800s, and especially after the Napoleonic wars, which ended in 1815. She said that for the first time in human history, the expression *to make money* was developed. *Making money* meant that you could bring together resources, raw materials, labor, and eventually machinery, and you could actually create wealth where no wealth had existed before.

For a hundred years the U.S. was the preeminent place in the world for actually making money. You created money out of nothing. You grew stuff out of the ground or pulled stuff out of the ground. You took human labor, you cut down trees, you smelted the steel or wove the clothing. You created the machinery. You created wealth from raw materials and labor.

A good friend of mine, who's now one of the richest men in the world, wrote a book. He said that *man's material welfare*, MMW, is the equivalent of tools times time or money. He basically said that man's material welfare comes from tools, which cost an enormous amount of money to develop, multiplied times labor. This has never really changed.

Today, to create one job in retail costs $100,000, and to create one job in petrochemical engineering costs $500,000. To create a job in every single industry, there's an amount of money that has to be invested. That amount of money has to be invested by someone who has saved it from expenditure. Capitalism is really "savings-ism": wherever there are high levels of savings, there are high levels of capital available to be invested in new businesses and opportunities, which can create wealth and jobs and can create possibilities for the future.

Creating wealth means that you're finding new ways to serve other people. You're finding ways to enhance the lives and work of other people in such a way that they will willingly, eagerly pay you for your product or service. Then simultaneously you have to compete, because everybody else wants the same customers, because they also want to create the same wealth and they also want to enjoy the same standards of living.

The abundance mentality says there are unlimited opportunities, because human beings have unlimited wants. This is one of the most important principles I've ever learned. As long as there are human wants unfulfilled and human problems unsolved and human needs that have not been taken care of, there will always be opportunities for the creative minority.

Dan

One thing that often keeps people from creating tremendous wealth is the level of risk to which they must expose themselves. Discuss the risk that must be taken to achieve the highest, category-defining levels of success, like that of Mark Zuckerberg, Warren Buffett, or Sara Blakely, founder of Spanx. Is it worth taking that level of risk? Can people who have more modest aspirations still create tremendous value?

Brian

Let's take the three examples. Mark Zuckerberg came up with this idea in his dorm room of linking boys and girls at Harvard by putting their profiles up on a website. You saw a girl or a guy, you'd go and check them out.

They called it the Facebook. People could go and check the faces of people at Harvard. It was a great idea. More people started to do it, and people started to come on. They wouldn't make any money at it at all; it was just a project for the geeks. Pretty soon everybody at Harvard was on it, because if you wanted to be socially active, if you wanted people to know about you and what you're interested in, you would go on this site. People started to share messages back and forth. It was so successful at Harvard that someone from Yale said, "Can you do a Yale Facebook?" They said, "Sure." So they took the same technology and used it to create another Facebook.

Then they realized that people who aren't at college would like this as well. It grew by accident. Everybody wanted to be able to communicate online with other people and share stories and pictures and so on. It was very primitive at the beginning, and it was just a fluke of luck that they happened to develop a technology that went viral. Imagine: there are 1.2 billion people on it now. As many as a billion people use Facebook each day. That is phenomenal. It was a real stroke of luck, because before Facebook there had been other social media sites. Myspace just disappeared.

Warren Buffett took a course at Columbia from a man named Ben Graham. Ben Graham was the father of value investing. He said that you have to look really deeply into the fundamentals of a company to find out if the product or service that it sells really generates value for the customer. They call this *value creation* and *value capture*. Value creation has to do with the customers, because the product enhances their lives greatly in excess of the amount money they pay. Value capture is capturing part of the value that you create for other people.

Graham taught this philosophy of looking at businesses in terms of their underlying value and how these companies offered greater or better or different value than their competitors in similar industries. Simultaneously, he asked, who were the people in the company? Were they good managers? Were they astute developers of new products? Were they ambitious and always looking for ways to improve the product? There was and is a combination of value creation factors.

Warren Buffett grew up in a nice family. His father was stationed in Washington, and when Warren was about fourteen years old, they didn't have much money, so he got a job delivering newspapers in the morning. He got one penny for every newspaper he delivered. He was careful with his money, so his parents paid all of his expenses. For the next two years he delivered more than 200,000 newspapers, getting up at four in the morning, delivering papers, coming home, going to school.

He saved $2000, graduated from Columbia, and with his $2000 he started his business. He followed Ben Graham's idea: invest in companies that are valuable, and offer products and services that people like and want and which are considered superior to the competitors' products, and which generate profits. Then take those profits and channel them into buying other companies that are also selling products or services that people want and are generating profits. Then take that larger profit stream and repeat. He kept doing that to the point where today he's the most successful investor in history.

It's a very simple concept. Buffett took the course accidentally with Ben Graham, but it set him at a young age. It gave him the fixed idea of how to invest, and he never deviated from that idea. All over America and the world there are now what they call *Buffett billionaires*. These were people, doctors, lawyers, salespeople, business owners in Omaha that knew Warren. He was a nice young guy in his twenties, starting off investing his own $2000, and did pretty well. So they said, "Warren, would you invest my money as well?" He said, "Sure." You never hear of these people, but some of them are worth $5 billion and $6 billion, because they got in with Warren when he was a young guy investing money.

Now let's take Sara Blakely, who invented Spanx. She had the same concern that many women have, which is, they want to look good. She looked around and found that there were all kinds of undergarments for women, but none that were using the kind of plasticized technology that was available that would actually make them look firm. She found that no one else was doing this. That's how Sara Blakely started Spanx.

They had a variety of different products, and she came up with some great ideas. She developed her own models and had them manufactured. Then she had to go from store to store and get the stores and boutiques to sell them on consignment. Finally people started to buy them, and it started to take off. At the very beginning she had to work her bum off, if you like, to get people to carry the product, but it turned out to be the right product at the right time.

She was a smart businesswoman, she got really good designers, and she still designs every product herself. As a result the company went ballistic, because there are so many people who wanted the product, and she had such a great quality product. Today Spanx is the best. It's considered the highest-quality product.

It's the same as Apple iPhones. People will pay much more for an iPhone than for a Samsung or some other phone, because the iPhone is considered to be the premium product in the market. There's always a huge market for the premium product.

Dan

Brian, what should people take home from this discussion of creating wealth?

Brian

The most important principle of all has to do with continuous improvement. Have you heard the formula CANEI, which stands for *continuous and never-ending improvement?*

The greatest enemy of success, both financially and in every other area, is complacency, the lure of the comfort zone. Many companies will come out of the gate with a great product. The product receives tremendous market acclaim, they sell a whole pile of it, and then the competitors will pile in. It's an economic principle: wherever there are higher-than-average potential profits, competitors will rush in with similar products or services to try to get a piece of those extra profits. I wrote an article on this many years ago that was published in all the newspapers, called "The Only Cure for High Prices Is High Prices." People always complain when prices go up. Don't worry, because competitors will rush into the market and will create much more of the product. There will be an oversupply, and then the prices will drop. They'll crash because people will be trying to move their overstocks. So the higher the price, the faster competitors come in, the more they produce, and the lower the eventual price.

But continuous and never-ending improvement is the reason why some companies and individuals are incredibly successful. Every day in every way I'm getting better and better. I'm learning more. I never go to sleep at night without knowing more than I knew when I got up in the morning. Successful individuals are always listening to audio programs and reading and upgrading their skills.

I just got a message from my business partner, who's been out of town for three days attending a very high level seminar workshop on digital marketing, which we have a great business in. He is so excited. Some of the smartest people in the country are sharing concepts in digital marketing that increase response rates, sales rates, repurchase rates. He is always going to these courses, and he's built one of the most successful digital online marketing businesses in the country.

It's no miracle. Continuous and never-ending improvement is the reason why companies get better and better, and make their products faster and better and cheaper and easier and more convenient. If you keep pushing forward, constantly looking for ways to improve, you're going to hit something like a Spanx or a Facebook or a Microsoft. You're going to hit something that nobody has ever seen before. It's because you're way out in front, taking risks, pushing the outer edge of the envelope, always looking for ways to make it better and better and better.

At a certain point, God willing and the river don't rise, as they say, if you're really fortunate, you could break through. That's how people go from struggling to becoming billionaires within one generation.

SEVEN

The Science of Multiplying Wealth

Once you have achieved a certain level of financial success, you will want to find a way to invest your money so you can multiply it many times over while you are busy working on becoming even more successful in your chosen profession. But as we will see, some people make the mistake of risking too much when investing, either because they are ill-informed, too greedy, or too busy to pay sufficient attention to where and how they are investing.

In this chapter Brian will teach you the science of multiplying wealth—what has been proven to work with the greatest number of people over the greatest period of time. Some people resist the idea that there could be a science of multiplying wealth, especially when there is no guaranteed rate of return for any investment. Yet, as Brian will show you, this view that investing doesn't have principles that have proven to work is just wrong. Not knowing these ideas can cost you a fortune.

Brian

One of your major goals in life should be financial independence. You must aim to reach the point where you have enough money so that you never have to worry about money again. The good news is that financial independence is easier to achieve today than it has ever been before. We live in the richest country at the richest time in all of human history, irrespective of short-term economic ups and downs. We're surrounded by more wealth and affluence than ever before.

As I told you, when I started off there were a million million-aires and a few billionaires. Now there are 10 million millionaires and 2000 billionaires. The billionaires are increasing at the rate of forty or fifty a year, which is an incredible amount of money. One thousand million dollars starting from nothing!

Your goal should be to participate fully in what many people are starting to refer to as the golden age of mankind.

Money has an energy of its own, and it's largely attracted to people who treat it well. Money tends to flow toward those people who can use it in the most productive ways to produce valuable goods and services and to those who can invest it to create employment and opportunities that benefit others. At the same time, money flows away from those who use it poorly or who spend it in nonproductive ways. Your job is to acquire as much money as you honestly can and then to use it to enhance the quality of your life and the lives of those you care about.

Let's talk about some of the laws of money. The first is the *law of cause and effect*, which says that everything happens for a reason. There is a cause for every effect. This is the iron law of human destiny. This law says that we live in a world governed by law, not by chance. Everything happens for a reason, whether we know what it is or not. Every effect, success or failure, wealth or poverty, has a specific cause or causes. Every cause or action has an effect or a consequence of some kind or another, whether we can see it or not or whether we like it or not.

This law says that all achievement, all wealth, all happiness, all prosperity, all success are the direct and indirect effects or results of specific causes or actions. This means that if you can be clear about the effect or result you want, you can probably achieve it. You can study others who have accomplished the same goal, and by doing what they did, you could get the same results.

The law of cause and effect applies to money as much as to any other subject. This law says that financial success is an effect. As such, it proceeds from certain specific causes. When you identify these causes and implement them in your life and activities, you will get the same effects that hundreds of thousands, and even millions, of others have gotten. You can acquire whatever amount of money you really want if you will just do what others have done before you to achieve the same results. And if you don't, you won't.

It's as simple as that.

Your ultimate financial goal should be to accumulate capital until your investments are paying you more than you can earn on your job. This is your basic goal in life. The sooner you set it as a goal and the sooner you work on it, the sooner you're going to achieve it.

Let's talk about the next law, which is called the *law of investing*. The law of investing says, investigate before you invest. This is one of the most important of all the laws of money. You should spend at least as much time studying a particular investment as you do earning the money to put into that investment. Never let yourself be rushed into parting with money. You have worked too hard to earn it and have taken too long to accumulate it.

Investigate every aspect of the investment well before you make any commitment. Ask for full and complete disclosure of every detail. Demand honest, accurate, and adequate information on any investment of any kind. If you have any doubt or misgivings at all, you will probably be better off keeping your money in the bank or in a money market account than you would taking the risk of losing it.

The first corollary of the law of investing is that the only thing easy about money is losing it. It's hard to make money in a competitive market, but losing it is one of the easiest things you can ever do. A Japanese proverb says making money is like digging with a nail, while losing money is like pouring water on the sand.

The second corollary of this law comes from the self-made multibillionaire Marvin Davis, who was asked about his rules for making money in an interview in *Forbes* magazine. He said he has one simple principle, and it is, *don't lose money*. He calls this rule number one. He said that if there's a possibility that you will lose your money, don't part with it in the first place. This principle is so important that you should write it down and put it where you can see it. Read it and reread it over and over.

Think of your money as if it were a piece of your life. You have to exchange a certain number of hours and weeks and even years of your time in order to generate a certain amount of money for savings or investment. That time is irreplaceable. It's a part of your precious life that is gone forever. If all you do is to hold on to the money rather than losing it, that alone can assure that you achieve financial security. Don't lose money.

The third corollary of the law of investing says that if you think you can afford to lose a little, you're going to end up losing a lot.

There's something about the attitude of the person who feels that he has enough money that he can afford to risk losing a little. You remember the old saying, a fool and his money are soon parted. There's another saying that says, when a man with experience meets a man with money, the man with the money is going to end up with the experience, and the man with the experience is going to end up with the money.

So always ask yourself, what would happen if you lost 100% of a prospective investment? Could you handle that? If you couldn't, don't make the investment in the first place.

The fourth corollary of the law of investing says, only invest with experts who have a proven track record of success with their own money. Your aim is to invest only with people who have such a successful track record with money that your risk is dramatically diminished. Again, don't lose money. If ever you feel tempted, refer back to this rule and resolve to hold on to what you have.

Invest only in things that you fully understand and believe in. Take investment advice only from people who are financially successful from taking their own advice. By the way, when the market turns down, many people who offer financial advice are broke and homeless and unemployed and working at McDonald's. Many people who sell financial success products or get-rich-quick products have no other money than the money that they get from selling these products to unsuspecting people who think it's possible to make easy money.

The next law is the *law of compound interest.* This says that investing your money carefully and allowing it to grow at compound interest will eventually make you rich. Compound interest is considered to be one of the great miracles of all of human history and economics. Albert Einstein described it as the most powerful force in our society, if not in the universe. When you let money accumulate at compound interest over a long enough period of time, it increases more than you could imagine.

You can use the rule of 72 to determine how long it would take for your money to double at any rate of interest. You simply divide the interest rate into the number 72. For example, if you are receiving 8% interest on your investment and you divided the number 72 by 8, you would get the number 9. This means that it would take you nine years to double your money at 8% interest. It's been estimated that one dollar invested at 3% interest at the time of Christ would be worth half the money in the world today. If the money had been allowed to grow and double and double again and then again and again and again, it would be worth many billions or trillions of dollars today.

So the first corollary of this law says the key to compound interest is to put the money away and never touch it. Once you begin accumulating money and it begins to grow, you must never touch it or spend it for any reason. If you do, you lose the power of compound interest, even though you spend only a small amount today, you'll be giving up what could be an enormous amount later on.

If you start early enough, invest consistently enough, never draw on your funds, and rely on the miracle of compound interest, it will make you rich. An average person earning an average income who invested $100 per month from age twenty-one to age sixty-five and who earned a compounded rate of interest of 10% over that time would retire with a net worth of $1,118,000.

Begin a regular monthly investment account and commit yourself to investing a fixed amount for the next five, ten, or even twenty years. Select a company with a family of mutual funds and investment instruments. Keep your money working month after month and year after year.

The next law of money is the *law of accumulation*. This says that every great financial achievement is an accumulation of hundreds of small efforts and sacrifices that no one ever sees or appreciates. The achievement of financial independence will require a tremendous number of small efforts on your part. To begin the process of accumulation, you must be disciplined and persistent. You must keep at it for a long, long time. Initially you will see very little change or difference, but gradually your efforts will begin to bear fruit. You will begin to pull ahead of your peers. Your finances will improve, and your debts will disappear. Your bank account will grow, and your whole life will improve.

The first corollary of the law of accumulation says that as your savings accumulate, you develop a momentum that moves you more rapidly towards your financial goals. It's hard to get started on a program of financial accumulation, but once you do, you find it easier and easier to keep at it. The *momentum principle* is one of the great success secrets. This principle says that it takes tremendous energy to get started and to overcome the initial inertia and resistance to financial accumulation, but once started, it takes much less energy to keep moving.

The second corollary of the law of accumulation says, by the yard it's hard, but inch by inch anything's a cinch. When you first begin thinking about saving 10% or 20% of your income, you'll immediately think of all kinds of reasons why it's not possible. You may be up to your neck in debt, you may be spending every single penny that you earn just to keep afloat.

However, if you find yourself in this situation, there's a solution. Begin saving just 1% of your income in a special account, which you refuse to touch. Begin putting your change into a large jar every evening when you come home. When the jar is full, take it to the bank and add it to your savings account. Whenever you get an extra sum of money from selling something—an old debt is repaid or a bonus comes unexpectedly—instead of spending it, put it into your special account. These small amounts will begin to add up at a rate that will surprise you. As you become comfortable with saving 1%, increase it to 2%, then 3%, then 4%, and 5% and so on. Within a year you'll find yourself getting out of debt and saving 10% to 15%, even 20% of your income without it really affecting your lifestyle.

The next law of money is called the *law of magnetism*. This says that the more money you save and accumulate, the more money you attract into your life. The law of magnetism, often called the *law of attraction*, has been a primary reason for wealth building throughout history. This law explains much of the success and failure in every area of life, especially in the financial arena. Money goes where it is loved and respected. The more positive emotions you associate with your money, the more opportunities you will attract to acquire even more.

The first corollary of the law of magnetism as it applies to money is that a prosperity consciousness attracts money like iron filings to a magnet. This is why it is so important for you to start accumulating money, no matter what your situation. Put just a few coins into a piggy bank. Begin saving even a small amount of money. That money, magnetized by your emotions of desire and hope, will begin to attract more to you faster than you could imagine.

The second corollary of this law says it takes money to make money. As you begin accumulating money, you begin to attract more money, and more opportunities to earn money, into your life. This is why it's so important to start even with a small amount. You'll be amazed at what starts to happen. Take time every day, every week, and every month to reflect on your financial situation and look for ways to deploy your finances more intelligently.

As we said before, self-made millionaires think more about financial accumulation in a ratio of 10:1 to poor people. Every week they take time to think about how much they have, how it's deployed, and how they can earn more, and how they can invest it better. The more time you take to think intelligently about your finances, the better decisions you will make and the more money you will have to think about. And the more you think about your savings and investments, the more of them you will attract into your life.

Another law is called the *law of accelerating acceleration*. This says that the faster you move toward financial freedom, the faster it moves toward you. The more money you accumulate and the more success you achieve, the faster money and success seem to move towards you, from a variety of different directions.

Everyone who is financially successful today has had the experience of working extremely hard, sometimes for years, before they got their first real opportunity, but after that, more and more opportunities flowed to them from all directions. The major problem most successful people have is in sorting out the opportunities that seem to come at them from everywhere. It will be the same for you.

Look at the companies in Silicon Valley who invested millions and then tens of millions and then hundreds of millions. They invested in companies like Facebook and Google and Apple, and they made hundreds of millions and billions of dollars. Now opportunities come to them like rivers from all directions to invest in places where they'll make hundreds of millions of dollars more.

Peter Lynch, former manager of the Fidelity Magellan Fund, one of the most successful mutual funds in history, said that the best investments he ever made were those that took a long time to come to fruition. He would often buy the stock of a company that did not increase in value for several years. Then it would take off and go up ten or twenty times in price. This strategy of picking stocks for the long term, the Warren Buffett strategy, eventually made him one of the most successful and highest-paid money managers in America.

This brings us to the *law of the stock market*. The value of a stock today is the total anticipated cash flow of that stock discounted to the present day. What does this mean? It means that a share of stock represents a share of the ownership of the company. This entitles the owner of the share to all the benefits and risks of ownership, including profits, losses, stock increases, declines in value, good or poor management, and increasing or decreasing demands for the products or services produced and sold by the company. When you buy a share of stock, you are an owner of everything that takes place in that company. When you buy a stock, you are investing a certain sum of money and betting that your return will be in excess of what you could earn in a guaranteed investment such as a bond or a money market fund.

Purchasing this stock is a form of gambling, because the future of the company and the value of the stock are both unpredictable. They are determined by countless market forces such as sales, competition, technological change, interest rates, quality of management, world events, weather, and many other factors.

The first corollary of the stock market is that bulls make money, and bears make money, but pigs get slaughtered. This means that people who invest aggressively when the market is rising make money. People who sell short and protect themselves when the market is declining make money. But greedy people who try to make a killing in the market almost always lose money.

More than 70% of day traders or flash traders today, people who move in and out of the market completely one day at a time or sometimes one hour at a time, lose money. Many of them lose everything.

The second corollary is that long-term investing in the American stock market is the best way to achieve long-term financial security. The value of stocks traded on the U.S. markets has increased an average of 11% over the past eighty years. As a result, a person who began investing at the age of twenty and who invested $100 per month in a mutual fund that increased an average of 10% per year would retire with a net worth of more than $1 million.

The third corollary is that dollar cost averaging over the long run will make you rich. This corollary means that market timing doesn't work. It is virtually impossible for you or anyone to consistently buy stocks when the prices are low and sell them when the prices are high. It's always better to buy the stocks of a good, solid company selling valued and respected products and services and then hold on to those stocks for the long run. This is called *value investing*, and it's what makes people in the stock market wealthy.

Corollary number four says the stock market is managed and made by professionals. This means that every purchase of a stock represents the sale of that same stock by someone else. The person purchasing the stock is betting that the stock will increase in price. The person selling the stock is betting that the stock will decline in price. Every stock purchase and sale is there for a zero-sum game, with one person betting his wisdom and judgment against that of another person.

Most of these people are professionals who do this for fifty to sixty hours each week and sometimes for several decades. This means that your safest course of action is to invest in an index fund that represents all of the stocks in that index and which goes up or down based on the average trend of the entire market. The most popular type of index fund is the Standard & Poor's 500, although there are many others. The Standard & Poor's index funds have consistently outperformed more than 80% of professionally managed mutual funds over the years.

The next law of investing is the *law of real estate*. This law says that the value of a piece of real estate is the future earning power of that particular piece of property. The value of any piece of property is determined by the income that can be generated by that property when it is developed to its highest and best use from this moment onward into the future. A piece of property may have sentimental value to a particular owner, but its dollar value is directly related to its future earning power.

There are millions of acres of land that will never have any value, like desert land, for instance, which has no future earning power. It cannot be developed to produce income, provide accommodation, or satisfy any particular human needs. There are vast areas in many large cities where property values are declining. For instance, think about Detroit, where growth and development have come and gone and will probably not return. Every day men and women are selling homes and properties at less than they paid for them or are losing them to foreclosure, because these properties have declined in earning power, in rental power, and therefore in value.

The first corollary of the law of real estate is that you make your money when you buy and you realize it when you sell. This is very important. It is by purchasing a piece of property at the right price and under the right terms that enables you to sell it at a profit. Many people think that they'll make their money when they sell the property, irrespective of how they purchased the property or at what price. This is getting the cart before the horse. The more carefully you investigate a piece of property and the more thoroughly you prepare a purchase offer, the more likely it is that you will get the kind of deal that will enable you to sell that property at a profit later on.

The second corollary of the law of real estate is, the three keys to real estate selection are location, location, location. Each piece of property is unique in that there's only one piece of property like that on the earth's surface. Your ability to choose a piece of property in an excellent location will have more of an impact on the future earning power of that property than almost any other decision that you make.

The third corollary of the law of real estate is that real estate values are largely determined by general economic activity in the area and by the number of jobs and the level of wages. This is very important when you're selecting a neighborhood or a community in which to invest. Generally speaking, the value of property increases at three times the rate of population growth and two times the rate of inflation. When you purchase property in a fast-growing community, you are virtually ensured of above-average increases in value.

For example, today in Santa Clara and around Silicon Valley, because of the incredible explosion of employment and high tech, high paying businesses, real estate values have increased five and ten times over what they were a few years ago. The most important factors affecting the value of real estate in any area are the level of new business formation and economic growth in the surrounding area. Make a decision today to purchase a piece of real estate for investment purposes. The only way you can learn about real estate investing is by actually becoming an owner and then by putting your knowledge and skills to work to increase the value of that piece of property.

Once upon a time, there was a man named Bernard Baruch, who at the beginning of the twentieth century started off as a stock market runner, running orders back and forth from stockbrokers. But while most of his friends were playing around, he would ask the people that he was delivering purchase or sale orders to about why they were making that decision. Over time, he got a sense for what made a good stock market investment, and he began to invest a dollar a week.

Within a few years, he was one of the richest men in America. He was an advisor to six presidents. He wrote books and articles. At the end of his life, he summarized what he called the ten rules for investment success, and I'll finish off this section by reading them to you.

Rule number one is, don't speculate unless you can make it a full-time job. Remember, every decision you make is a bet against the decision of someone else who is studying the stock market forty, fifty, sixty hours a week, as I've mentioned.

Number two, beware of anyone bringing gifts of inside information or tips. The number one way to lose money in the stock market is to act on tips from people who really don't know what they are talking about, like taxi drivers, bartenders, barbers, and even your close friends at work.

Rule number three, before you buy a security, find out everything you can about the company, its management and competitors, its earnings and possibilities for growth. Be patient and disciplined, objective, and unemotional. As we said, take the time to investigate before you invest.

Rule number four, don't try to buy at the bottom and sell at the top. This can't be done, except by liars. When you buy a stock, decide at what price you will sell it, and when it hits that price, don't be greedy. With program and computer trading today, you can set a sell price on a stock that will be triggered automatically when it hits that price. You will never go broke taking a profit.

Rule number five, learn how to take your losses quickly and cleanly. Don't expect to be right all the time. If you have made a mistake and you see that the stock is going down, sell the stock and cut your losses as quickly as possible.

Rule number six, don't buy too many different securities. Better to have only a few investments which can be watched than to have too many. Diversification spreads your risk, but it also eliminates any chance you might have for major gains if one of your stocks were to increase rapidly in value. This is a rule for people who are going to trade in the stock market, not for the average person, who is much better off buying an index fund and just holding it.

Rule number seven, make a periodic reappraisal of all your investments and see whether changing developments have altered their prospects. Use zero-base thinking. Always ask when you have new information, "If I had not already purchased this stock or investment, knowing what I now know, would I purchase it again today?" If the answer is no, that is your cue to sell.

Rule number eight, study your tax position to know when you can sell to greatest advantage. Be aware of the capital gains taxes that are applicable to your transactions. Remember that the only thing that counts is the amount that you have left after taxes. The timing of stock market purchases and sales to create capital gains and capital losses is an area with which you should be thoroughly familiar.

Rule number nine, always keep a good part of your capital in a cash reserve. Never invest all your funds. If you keep a cash cushion at all times, you will also be in a position to take advantage of unexpected opportunities that come along. You will also have an emergency reserve to act as a buffer, no matter what happens in the marketplace.

Rule number ten, don't try to be a jack of all investments. Stick to the field you know best. Warren Buffett said the same thing. He never invested in dot-com or Internet stocks, he said, "because I just don't understand them or how they're valued." And he never lost money, while everybody else lost a fortune when the dot-com dot-bomb explosion took place. Usually the most successful investors are those who pick one particular industry and concentrate on becoming knowledgeable about the companies in that industry. Pick an industry that interests you, so that you'll enjoy keeping current with it.

Remember, the key to success in investing is to investigate before you invest. Invest carefully. Get all the information that you require. If you're going to be an active investor, you have to watch your money all the time. If you're not going to be an active investor, the best thing that you can do is buy an index fund that has a low cost of management and which will grow as the market moves. You can put it aside and sleep well at night and never worry.

EIGHT

The Science of Wealth Protection

Once you have become financially successful and have acquired a good level of wealth, your job is not over. The Science of Money approach requires you to install various forms of wealth protection so that you don't quickly lose what it took years to build.

Think of this approach like a pyramid in Egypt. You want your financial structure to be so strong that nothing, no financial storm of any kind, either your own storm or one in the national economy, can blow a hole in your financial foundation. This session will teach you the steps you need to take to construct your own financial pyramid.

Dan

Brian, let's begin this section by having you discuss your own experiences in life with losing money, be it the loss of a major client, being sued in business, or taking a huge hit in the stock market. What lessons did you learn from these experiences? How did they convince you of the importance of a proper plan for wealth protection?

Brian

I spent much of my life achieving financial independence. Then you develop the *walk-on-water syndrome*. It's very common, and it's the major reason why people go astray later on in life.

We spend most of our lives developing our skills and abilities, building our businesses, and accumulating wealth. Then, later on in life, we can make a series of mistakes. One of the worst of all is the walk-on-water syndrome. We make a lot of money by becoming very, very good over an extended period of time in our own field. We think, "I'm so good that I can transfer that knowledge, ability, skill, confidence to some other area, and I can do equally well in that area."

When the real estate market was booming back in the 2000s, somebody approached me and said, "There's tremendous opportunity to build self-storages in these fast-growing communities, because they fill up like rain barrels in the springtime and they cast off a very high level of cash flow, they increase in value, and all will be well."

So I said, "Sure, why not? Sounds like a good idea." He had some good contacts, he was doing a lot of work, he put together some financial proposals. It sounded very good, so I began to invest. A little bit in the beginning, and then more and more, until I invested about $20 million in self-storages. It wasn't all my money, but it was all leveraged off of investments that I made.

It turned out that he'd never done it before and that the figures that he projected to me weren't true. They left out interest payments, they left out an enormous number of fundamental costs, which I wasn't able to recognize, because it wasn't my area of expertise. I ended up completing the self-storages and selling them at massive losses and losing a lot of money.

My favorite two words in all of wealth protection are *due diligence*. This means to carefully investigate every single detail of an investment. Double-check, get experts to look at it, speak to accountants, bankers, speak to people in the industry. Go completely around the people that you are doing business with and get outside opinions. If I had done that just a little, I would have saved myself, not only an enormous amount of time, but an enormous amount of lost money that I would have accumulated over time.

If you want to maintain your wealth, if you want to protect your wealth, be very cautious and careful about what you do with the money once you attain it.

The best thing of all is to invest with experts. I was just talking to a man the other day who works in wealth management. He works for families that have a net worth of $25 million or more. They turn over all their investments to him and his company, and he takes care of every single part of their financial lives, from bank accounts to credit cards to mortgages to savings accounts to loans to home equity. And, of course, investing. Because he and his company are so sophisticated, they generate 10–20% per year return on their investments, and their clients get richer and richer, because they can afford to pay them. Usually they charge about 1% as the total management fee for the amount.

If the amount goes up or the investment goes up, it's 1% across the board. They generate very high returns, which the average person can't do. The average person has to realize that the only thing that's easy about money is losing it. If you're going to accumulate money, at a certain point in life, probably around the age of fifty, you have to start gearing back down again.

You could take a lot of risks when you're younger, you can really work hard and be aggressive, but at the age of fifty you start to step it down a bit and start to be more cautious and more careful. And you remember the rule, don't lose money. If you have the slightest possibility that you're going to lose money, just stop and say, "Wait a minute, can I afford to lose all this money?" If the answer is no, don't do it.

Dan

Do you find that it is true that the more successful, financially and otherwise, you become, the more of a target you become for lawsuits, failed business deals, etc.? Why or why not?

Brian

One problem that we have in the U.S. today is we have too many lawyers and too little work for them. So there are lawyers who go out and try to create work by suing people. I call these used-car-salesman lawyers, garbage lawyers, bottom-of-the-barrel-scraping lawyers.

Because they are so powerful in Congress and in the state legislatures, they've passed laws that enable them to sue with no basis at all. So the rule is that if you have money, you're going to be sued. A friend of mine, who is quite wealthy, said, "If you have money, you're going to be sued four times." You just have to take in a deep breath and recognize that if you have something to go after, the lawyers will go after it on straight commission.

Now here's what I also found out: if somebody sues you, you have to defend yourself. It may cost $75,000 or $100,000, but if you are sued, you must defend or they get a summary judgment against you, and you will be found to be 100% guilty. If you want to fight, you have to go through depositions, you have to hire lawyers, you have to subpoena and grill witnesses, you'll have to do a whole lot of things that are part of the process.

If you don't do any of these things, then you don't have a sufficient defense. A person can sue you by paying $250. I have had every experience where people have sued me because they could. The basis was completely fraudulent. But the lawyers are hungry. I found out about this one lawyer whom you would go to if you ever wanted to sue somebody. He put in a standard form. He put in the name of the plaintiff, and your name at the top of the page, and his at name at the bottom, and he filed it for $250. Now you had to hire a lawyer and defend yourself.

I learned this from a very successful man some years ago: He said, "Put all of your assets into a family-limited trust, and set it up in such a way that it belongs to your family, but you have total management over the amount." You want to put your money in a place where can't be touched. If you put it into a family-limited trust and the person tries to sue you, the first thing the lawyers will do is see how much money you have. If they find it's in a family-limited trust, they'll walk away, because they know they can't get at it.

Let's say they get a judgment for $1 million against you. If it's a family-limited trust that you manage, you can say, "OK, you've got a judgment. I can determine how this money will be paid. We have decided by majority vote in the family-limited trust that we will pay it out at the rate of $10 per year until it's all paid back." They know you can do that, so they won't even sue you at all. They just walk away. It's a very good tactic, because we live in such a litigious society and because there are so many lawyers who are desperate for any kind of income. They will sue you on any basis if they think they can shake you down.

It's very important that you protect yourself, that you put your assets into trusts, family-limited trusts. Your lawyers and accountants can show you exactly what to do.

Dan

There are many tools for protecting yourself and your family. Let's begin by discussing a few. The first is insurance. What forms of insurance should everyone have? And what general rules should they be following when purchasing such insurance? For example, life insurance. Research shows term insurance is generally best versus whole life insurance for most people. Please include some other ideas about car insurance, home insurance, and even disability. Many people also say that today, with people living longer, you should consider obtaining long-term care insurance. Do you agree?

Brian

I believe that during your working lifetime, you should have life insurance. You should have just straight term insurance, where you buy the maximum amount for the lowest amount that you can pay. You should not have whole life or any kind of accumulative insurance, because these are what they call *forced savings*. Most of the money for the first three to five years on a whole life policy goes in straight commission to the agent.

Today most people use the expression "buy term and invest the difference." You can get a much better return if you just buy straight term and put whatever other money you were going to pay into an index fund. Your return will be far, far greater.

But you should have enough insurance to protect your family if something should happen to you. A good friend of mine, a great insurance agent, said that the purpose of life insurance is to guarantee your dreams. If your dreams are that your spouse will be provided for and your kids will be able to go to school, even if something happens to you, you buy enough insurance to cover that.

You calculate how much would it take to provide for your spouse for the rest of her life if something were to happen to you. Most men think like this, but my friend said that during your lifetime, your job is to reach the point where you don't need life insurance, because you have already accumulated enough so that she has that protection.

As you get older, the cost of insurance becomes absolutely outrageous. If you buy $1 million worth of life insurance in your seventies, you may have to pay $500,000 a year for it. It's very, very expensive. So it doesn't make any sense. Your job is to accumulate enough money and then put the money aside so it cannot be touched. It cannot be touched by creditors, it cannot be touched by lawsuits, it can't be touched for any reason at all, so that you can provide for your dreams.

Dan

What do you feel about disability insurance?

Brian

I do not take a stand on disability insurance. The life insurance companies love to sell it, because they have such high commissions for the agents. But I think if you properly insure, which you can through medical insurance and general blanket insurances, you can probably cover yourself for disability.

I really don't know enough about the subject. I only know that the life insurance agents are very aggressive about selling disability, so it's a very high-profit insurance for them. Especially since fewer and fewer people buy whole life—almost everybody buys term—and the commissions on term policies are very low.

Dan

Brian, what do you feel about long-term care insurance for when we get older?

Brian

It's probably a good idea, for two reasons. Your children may not be able to take care of you. If you can make sure that you will live in a nice facility for the rest of your life, it's a very smart thing to do. The earlier you do it, of course, the better the rates you can get, because long-term care insurance is based on how long they think you will live once you go into a long-term care facility. After all, their goal is to make a profit. Therefore investigate it very carefully. Look at it, get the opinions of people you respect. Financial advisors and even a good insurance agent will tell you what is good for you and what is not.

It's the same with disability insurance. There are some policies that have low deductibles but are very expensive. Some have higher deductibles and they're much cheaper. Just like collision insurance for your car. If you have a deductible that's $1000, your insurance is going to be much less than if you have a $250 or a $500 deductible.

These are things that a good insurance agent can guide you through. I said earlier that for twenty-eight years I've had a good insurance agent who looks at every single insurance need and proposal and passes judgment on it from our point of view—what the best choice would be based on our unique situation. It's just like deciding what vitamins you should take, which sort of exercise regimen you need. It very much depends upon you and your situation, whether you're male or female, how much you're earning today, how much you have put aside. These are all factors that an expert can help you to work your way through.

Dan

Another tool for protecting you and your family is having a will. Discuss the importance of this tool.

Brian

It's very important that you do that. My wife and I have a will. We had one for some time, but then the executors changed, the children grew up, moved away, got married, had children; life changed. We wanted to be sure that our financial situation would be simplified. We went on to the LegalZoom website, and we downloaded a very simple will just to cover ourselves. We filled in the blanks and gave copies of it to our accountant and to our oldest children, so it's simple, clean, clear, uncomplicated.

Now we want to do a more detailed will. We'll go to an estate lawyer and have the lawyer walk us through twists and turns, because estate law is changing all the time. The government can come in and take more than 50% of your accumulated net worth. They can snatch it before there's any disposition or anything else, unless you provide against it. You need a lawyer who's current, literally almost up to the month, with the latest provisions in protecting yourself against hidden taxes.

The last thing you want is for an estate to destroy your family. They say there is nothing that so destroys a family than the disposition of an estate. I have seen this up close and personal, where several kids get along fine until a parent dies and leaves some money, and the money has to be divided up. The children—grown children now, in their thirties, forties, fifties—turn on each other like dogs fighting over pieces of meat. It destroys the whole family.

What a parent can do is to be very thoughtful about this. Before she died, my mother took every single item that she owned, every piece of furniture, every piece of jewelry, every piece of china, every piece of artwork, and she calculated its value. Then she allocated it amongst the four children. She picked my third brother, who is a lawyer, as executor.

When my mother died, we sat down and did the adjudication of the will. Everything was passed out, either on paper or physically. Then each grown child could exchange or barter items with the others. There was never an argument or disaffection for the rest of our lives, because my mother had thought things through carefully.

She didn't want people fighting over this or that. That's a very important thing that you do as a parent. You should start doing it by the time you're sixty or sixty-five. Planes run into mountains, and cars crash. You should protect your family by making sure that everything you ever accumulated is carefully handed out.

Another subject, which is becoming very hot today, is called *end-of-life discussions*. Once you reach sixty-five or seventy, you should open up the discussion—which your children won't like; they don't want to think about dying. But you should open up and say, "We will not be here forever, so if something were to happen to me, to him or her, or to both of us, these are some things that you might think about."

Open up the subject so it's not a hush-hush topic that people creep or tiptoe around, it's just an open subject, a normal and natural part of life. Then, even without the end-of-life discussion, they can say, as my kids do, "When you die, can I have this? Can I have that?"

It turns out that one daughter wants something that's really important to her. The son wants something else, and another child wants something else still. These are good things to get onto the table. It gives you a tremendous sense of peace and comfort to know that you've provided for all of this.

Dan

For employees, probably the most important thing is to protect their stream of income. What are the best things that employees can do to ensure that this stream of income is not interrupted? And if it is, what can they do so that it does not destroy them financially?

Brian

I have no idea how an employee who is earning a living and who loses a job for any reason can possibly protect himself against that loss of income, except by starting early and accumulating savings and having reserves of two to six months or more equal to their monthly income.

There's no insurance policy, there's no company policy, there's no other way that a person can do it, except by accepting personal responsibility and saying, "If something untoward were to happen, if I were to be incapacitated for a period of time, I have to have this amount of money put aside to provide for me, and the longer the better." One form of disability insurance that you can get is called *loss of income insurance*. You can say, "I need X number of thousand dollars per month." You can buy a policy for that amount in case you lose your job. However, the policy does not kick in for six to twelve months. They have no desire to give you that money back. You have to be either disabled or unable to work or unemployed or something for a long period of time before they'll finally start giving you those payments. Statistically they know that you'll probably be back at work well before that time.

Dan

For business owners, what are the different forms of incorporation, such as sole proprietorship, an LLC, an S corporation, etc.? What different forms of protection do they provide? How should one choose between them for a new business? Do you have any other ideas for how business owners can protect their wealth?

Brian

You or I could start a sole proprietorship right here. We could just name the company after ourselves, and we're in business. A sole proprietorship means that everything that we put into the company as an investment, everything we take out is taxable. It's like a complete flow-through corporation.

An S corporation is the same thing. With an S corporation, however, you could set up and take on debt, you could take out bank loans. You can hire staff, lease offices—you can run it just like a huge company, and still all the net income from the S corporation flows to the owners each year. I have an S corporation.

If you have 50% of the company and two other people have 25%, and the company earns $100,000, that money is automatic flow-through to your taxable income, and you must pay taxes on it.

A C corporation is different. A C corporation can accumulate money in the company, but you have to pay corporate taxes. Let's say your company earns $100,000. Corporate taxes in the U.S., the highest in the developed world, are about 39.5%. You'll have to pay 39.5%, and now you've got $60,500 left in the company.

If you pay that out as dividends to your shareholders, then they must pay their taxes at their own rates. And in the state of California, it's about 63% all in. It can be an enormous amount of money. However, you could leave the money in the company, which is what big companies like Apple do. They pay their taxes, and they've got $200 million sitting in the bank account, and they can do anything they want with that.

A C corporation is good if you're going to sell shares. You're going to have a large number of shareholders, and you're going to have investors invest with you and get a piece of the company. You also hope that the shares will increase in value. A C corporation is good for a larger company.

The challenge with the C corporation is that if you invest money in it and you lose the money, you cannot deduct it against your taxes. But if you invest money in a sole proprietorship or an LLC or an S corporation, that money can be deducted as a loss. The government allows you to deduct money that you spent in anticipation of earning a profit, except that money put into a C corporation is an investment. If the C corporation goes under, then you lose all the money that you invested in it without being able to deduct it. An LLC is a limited liability corporation. It's similar to a sole proprietorship or an S corporation. It's where two or three or more people get together. They put in their money and buy a piece of property, but all income can be taken out as investment, and all income flows through and is taxable for them.

Dan

Brian, if I'm starting a business, teach me how to choose between the three different types of incorporation—sole proprietorship, LLC, and an S corporation. What different types of legal protection do they provide?

Brian

I don't think there's really very much difference. It's really subtle. An LLC probably has subtle ways of accumulating capital, while a sole proprietorship is usually an individual operating on their own, but I do not think that there's any real tax advantage. It's very hard to avoid taxes in our system today. There are 84,000 pages of fine print to capture tax money from you at every single twist and turn. Taxes are almost impossible to avoid.

Again, the only thing that's really different is a C corporation, where you invest the money, but you can't get it out. You can lose it all. If you invest money in the other three, that is a cost of doing business and can be deducted as a loss against your current income.

NINE

The Science of
Money and Happiness

Our overview would not be complete without discussing the controversial topic of money and happiness. After all, what good is earning a great income and creating great wealth if it doesn't leave you happy and fulfilled as a human being? In this session, Brian will discuss some of the counterintuitive research on this topic. He will also tell you how to make sure that your own personal happiness increases as fast as your bank account.

Dan

Brian, let's begin by outlining how money and happiness are related. First, discuss the latest research that shows that more money provides more happiness up to around a middle-class level of existence—$50,000 a year household income, on average. Above that point additional money does not correlate well with an increase in happiness. What are your thoughts on these statistics? Do they line up with your own experience, moving from a very low income to great wealth?

Brian

One great discovery has to do with how people compare themselves with others. Nobody is either rich or poor except in comparison with other people within their community.

Leon Festinger of Harvard calls it *social comparison theory*. We look at people around us, and we compare ourselves with them. They just finished an experiment where they selectively gave people within a small, poor, village community a big chunk of money. Now they were wealthier than their neighbors, and it immediately made the neighbors envious and resentful. People who had been at their same level all the time suddenly had more money and could buy better things and have a slightly better standard of living. It made the others angry. But over time, the anger subsided, and feelings went back to neutral.

Researchers have also found that when people earn more money, they compare themselves upward. I remember my original goal way back in the '60s, when I started working, was to achieve $100,000. If I had $100,000—and of course, the money was worth much more at that time—I thought that I would really have succeeded. Then I began to meet other people who were worth substantially more. I got into investment sales. People invested $100,000, $250,000 with me, and the investment funds were worth millions.

Then I started to become aware of people who were living in million-dollar houses and had million-dollar incomes. So over time, unconsciously, I began to raise my standards for myself and to raise my aspirations. I looked at people earning more than me. You look for people that are about one or two steps ahead of you. You compare yourself with them, and you become discontent. But

I wasn't looking at people like Warren Buffett, who were earning billions.

So we compare ourselves upward. When people reach their first million dollars, they're happy, but then they start thinking about $2 million. They start looking upward at people who have $2 million. When you get to $2 million, you look at people who have $5 million. When you get to $5 million, you look at people who have $10 million. When you get to $10 million, you're looking at people who have $20 million.

People are always striving upward, and this really is a healthy thing. I call it *divine discontent.* You strive. Psychologists have found that your level of happiness or satisfaction is directly proportionate to where you are relative to where you thought you should be, or expected to be, at this stage of your life.

Interestingly, one of the highest levels of suicide takes place between the ages of forty-eight and fifty-two, mostly in men. It's because they realize that they're never going to make their great financial goals. They're not going to be millionaires. They're not going to be company owners. They're not going to be presidents of companies. For whatever reason, they realize that those aspirations have been dashed, and one day they go home and shoot themselves because of the incredible disappointment. They'd been fooling themselves for years into believing that a miracle was going to happen and suddenly they were going to make a quantum leap.

This is the philosophy of the lottery ticket: I can make mistakes all my life, but one lottery ticket is going to save me from a lifetime of not working, not upgrading my skills, not coming in early, not doing a good job. Somehow I'm going to be saved.

It's the same thing in Las Vegas. It's amazing, the number of poor people who go to Las Vegas, gambling away their grocery money, hoping that somehow that the cards are going to come up and the roulette wheel is going to turn, the slot machines are going to kick out the money, and they're going to be able to compensate for years and years of sloth.

Another thing to remember is that money doesn't make you happy. It's the feeling that you are accomplished at what you do, that you've been able to make this kind of money, that you've been able to provide this well for your family—that makes you happy. It's a feeling that you are fulfilling more and more of your potential, and here it's measurable. You can actually see the dollar measure.

Wealthy people will say that up to a certain point, money is just a measure of your ability to cover your cost of living and things like that. You strive for it. But after that point, you try to hold on to as much as possible by paying as little in taxes as possible, by protecting it, by preserving it, by doing due diligence. But it's not the money itself. It's just a measure.

You can be sure that Warren Buffett is not working for the money. He's working for the pleasure he gets from his work. The money is simply a measure of how well he's doing. If you're an investment advisor, that's a very good measure—how well you're doing for your clients—because that indicates how well you're doing for yourself.

So money becomes a measure and we judge ourselves against this measure.

Dan

In your experience, what is the biggest misconception that most people have about money and wealth as they relate to happiness?

Brian

Abraham Lincoln once said that a person is just about as happy as they make up their mind to be. Each person has a particular level of happiness. It's almost like a thermostat that's set at that level, and they keep going back to that level of happiness.

If a person wins a lottery, their happiness may spike for a period of time, but then it will go back to where it was before. Most people who invest in lottery tickets aren't very happy with their lives. So they invest in lottery tickets, and they win, and for a while, they're ecstatic about the money. The money goes through their fingers in about two years, and then they're just as miserable as they were before. It doesn't change their lives.

Other people will be pretty happy and then, say, they lose two legs in an accident. They'll go through the trauma of having lost two legs and being in a wheelchair for life. But, after about six to twelve months, they're just about as happy as they had been before the accident, and they're cheerful again. People have an automatic happy stat, if you like, and they keep going back to it.

The goal is to work on yourself and raise that level so that you're generally happy most of the time. This requires goals, hard work, becoming good at what you do, good relationships, health, and a whole lot of other things.

It's the decision you make, and that has a lot to do with your upbringing and your level of self-esteem, your self-concept. It has to do with a lot of things that are not controllable in the short term, but are controllable in the long term. You can do something about your personality. You can improve your self-confidence and self-esteem.

But generally speaking, people are at a given level of happiness. I look at my four children. They've been brought up with no criticism, high self-esteem, a lot of praise and encouragement, continuous validation by their parents, and they're happy whenever you see them. Anytime, anywhere, under any circumstances, no matter how much stress they have, they're generally happy and optimistic and cheerful, which means that upbringing really does make a difference.

Now if people have a certain standard of living that they're accustomed to, and their income drops and they can't afford that standard of living, that can make them really unhappy. The disparity between where they feel they should be and where they are can really cause them anger and frustration.

However, here's what happens. Each person has a self-concept level of income. If they go above their self-concept level of income by more than 10%, they engage in what we call *throwaway behaviors*. They start to gamble the money, spend it, go on vacations, somehow get rid of the money. If they earn 10% less than their self-concept level of income, they engage in scrambling behaviors. They start to work harder, work longer, upgrade their skills to get back into that comfort zone.

Another thing is that people choose their jobs and occupations by the way they like to receive money. There are two major ways in which people receive money. One is steady, dependable, consistent—weekly, two weeks, once a month, and so on. If you like safety, security, stability, a solid income, no surprises, no drama, then you seek a job that pays you money that way. This is the approach of the bulk of people who work today. They much prefer to have a steady secure income rather than to have income that fluctuates.

The other way of receiving money is in lumps, which is what entrepreneurs do. Entrepreneurs work six or seven months on putting together a deal, starting a business, turning it around. They'll have big spikes in income, and they're quite happy with that.

In Tom Stanley's book *The Affluent Society*, he said that the time to approach wealthy people is when they have their income spikes. If you're selling financial services, or property, or real estate, there's no point in talking to them in the slow season, when their business is down. If you ask when they have income spikes and they say, "I make all my money in the last three months of the year," then January is when you talk to those people. This is where they're at their peak of money and savings. This is when they're most open to investing, buying, purchasing something.

So that's a good question: how do you like to receive money? The other thing is your aspirations. If you're raised in a family with a lot of money, then your aspirations will be to duplicate that same level of income when you become an adult, and you're programmed to duplicate it. You're programmed to strive, to upgrade your skills, to work harder, to never be satisfied with a lower standard of living than you were brought up with. This is why so many people who come from entrepreneurial households become entrepreneurs and start their own businesses themselves. That's their worldview. That's their self-concept.

Dan

I think it was Earl Nightingale who said that becoming wealthy doesn't relieve you of your problems; you just have to deal with a whole new set of problems. So given that, obviously wealth is going to present some challenges or roadblocks, which, if not navigated well, can lead to unhappiness or even despair. Discuss some of these roadblocks that you've researched, or have experienced yourself, and how people can avoid or deal with them. Some that come to mind are less free time, less family time, higher levels of divorce—particularly for entrepreneurs—higher levels of stress or complexity due to increased possessions, more liability, etc.

Brian

Abraham Maslow, the great psychologist, said that we have two types of needs. There are *deficiency needs*, where we're trying to compensate for deficiencies—in safety, security, and belongingness. He said we also have *being needs*. We are trying to fulfill our potential. These needs have to do with self-esteem and self-actualization.

He said that 98% of people have deficiency needs. They are striving to compensate for feelings of inferiority, inadequacy, frustration, lack of happiness. They think if they achieve financial well-being, this will compensate for the aching, angry insecure feeling that they have inside, and they're always astonished when it doesn't.

One thing I began to teach a few years ago is summed up in a very simple statement: there is no joy in things. All joy comes from relationships. All joy comes from your interaction with other people. You may get joy from a sporting event or climbing a mountain or something like that, but you don't get joy from things.

A man could save his money and have an incredible year and go out and drive home with a $350,000 Silver Cloud Rolls-Royce. Then he parks in the driveway and walks in the house, and his wife is angry because he was supposed to have phoned a couple of hours ago and she didn't know whether to prepare the dinner. Now he's in an argument with her, and he forgets the car ever existed. In other words, the thing vanishes in your radar screen of what makes you happy or unhappy.

Another important thing about successful people is optimism. The founders of the most successful, fastest growing companies all have the quality of optimism. Researchers are amazed. Successful people have off-the-clock levels of optimism. They are so positive about themselves and their company.

Go back and ask, "Well, why did they start their company?" The answer was, because they really loved the product. So now they're spending all day long producing, selling, marketing, delivering, and seeing the results from their product. It makes them really happy. These people are working longer, harder hours, but they love to work at this. As a matter of fact, it is a deprivation to take them away from their work. It's a punishment.

My partner, Eric, and I joke about this—how we love to work. We have to use self-discipline not to work. Otherwise we'll just keep on working day and night and weekends, because we enjoy it so much. If you want to be successful, you have to deliberately decide to take time off. You have to schedule the time off, and you have to be adamant about not doing anything during that time until you get used to it. Spend time with your family. Spend time on health, walking, watching television, sports, but just take complete breaks. You have to work at it for a while. Then you're OK.

There's another important thing that I teach with regard to productivity. Completing a task gives you a feeling of energy, enthusiasm, and self-esteem. We're designed in such a way that being productive and getting results makes us happy. If we're being productive and getting results in our own business, it makes us happy. If we're earning money, we're selling products, we are moving ahead, our business is growing, our customers are happy, we're getting more customers, making more sales, it makes us happy all the time. It's mainlining happiness.

If you manage your time really well, you plan your days, and you work on your most important tasks, and then you complete those tasks, every time you do, you get a release of endorphins in your brain, which makes you happy. It gives you energy, makes you more personable, increases your creativity, strengthens your immune system. Many people who are doing something that they love really well, starting and completing tasks, are mainlining this happiness all the time.

Some may say, "These people are successful, but they're not happy." Well, we've done the research, and the fact is that successful people, rich people, are very happy. They just have a higher class of problems. Their higher class of problems is, which first-class restaurant do we go to? Do we order the filet mignon or the Australian lobster tail? When we go to Paris, do we stay at the George V, or at another first-class hotel that costs an outrageous fortune? Do we fly first-class, or business? These people have a different type of problem, but they are very happy, because they have freedom. They have the freedom to choose. They can say, "I can get this, or I can get that, because I have complete freedom to choose. I have enough money so that I don't have to deprive myself."

Here's another thing about self-made millionaires especially. When a man starts to make a lot of money in his own business or in anything else, his expenditures on himself, his clothing, his shoes, things like that, stay at the same level. They go up a little bit and flatten out, but his expenditures on his wife and children go up dramatically. Why? It's because men get tremendous joy from providing well for their families. They reach a certain level. One pair of shoes is enough; a couple of suits is enough. Men can just wear the same things and just dress it up by changing their tie or their shirt. Women like to have fifty pairs of shoes and a closet full of dresses.

There's a direct relationship between success and happiness, but it has to do with freedom, doing what you love, doing it well, being acknowledged, and then there is the score. The score is that you earn more money. And so, you could just say, "Boy, we're doing well. We had a great week, had a great month, had a great year, and we were successful," and success makes people happy.

Dan

This brings up the thought about providing for your children. Hopefully, all those people who are reading will give this book to their kids, so that they're able to learn these ideas and to get started on the right path financially.

But if you are someone who has worked hard and you've earned a great deal of money, you've had to go through all the work, all the trials and tribulations, to get to where you are. And then your kids are raised in relative luxury. Brian, what are some ideas that financially successful people can use to raise their children with the same sets of values and work ethic that they have?

Brian

That's a great question. What they found is that the sooner that children can make an association between effort and reward, especially financial reward, the more likely they are to be entre-preneurial. What I've done with my children is to give them an allowance, but ask them to do something for the allowance rather than just give them free money.

Some people say, "Children should be given allowances with no strings attached." That's not building children. What you do is, you say, "When you do this and this and you clean up your bedroom and put this away and empty the trash, then you get your allowance." They make an association between starting and completing tasks and earning money.

We live on the golf course of a very nice country club. We have a great slope to our house. The golfers would keep hitting golf balls up onto the slope. My kids would go out and pick up the golf balls and take them down and sell them back to the golfers as they came along. Sometimes, because our house is in a dogleg, golfers would try to loop the ball over the dogleg, and the balls would land in our yard. Our kids would go out and collect the balls, and then go down and sit by the golf course and sell them for two for a dollar to people going by.

The kids didn't need the dollars. Nonetheless, they made an association at the age of ten between working, getting the golf balls, going down, talking to the customers, and selling the golf balls. The golfers would come by, and they'd look at the golf balls and they'd pick the two that they wanted for a dollar. My sons would negotiate with them and come back with the dollars.

Each of my kids has had jobs as well, part-time jobs, when they were growing up, and they did that spontaneously. We have always taken them to the office. They come to the office, and they see us working; me and especially Barbara. They see that mom and dad are always working. It's an association between our standard of living and the fact that mom and dad work.

We talk to them about the work and about the business and about our staff. We include them as if they are full-time directors, or staff members, or shareholders, so that they get this feeling that they are part of a business enterprise.

These are all the things that you can do to avoid spoiling your children and having them grow up with no connection between hard work and reward.

Dan

Brian, to a certain degree, do you think that this whole concept of happiness as it relates to money is a bit overrated or even narcissistic? Even if there are periods of lesser happiness due to increased responsibility or stress, shouldn't the fact that you're creating wealth and improving the lives of others, taking part in something greater than just yourself, be a consideration as well?

Brian

Yes. People say, "You should do what you're passionate about. Do what makes a difference in the world and so on."

Now you have a whole generation of people who want to work in nonprofit activities. They want to do that because they're terrified of selling, because selling involves failure and, worst of all, rejection. People go into Internet businesses, because you can't be rejected when you send out a mass Internet mailing.

So an enormous number of people choose their occupation based on their psychological structure. One quality of healthy people is that they can take failure and rejection and bounce back. They have the quality of resilience. Therefore they're willing to try all kinds of things.

With regard to happiness, fulfillment, and so on, as I said before, successful people do what they love to do, and they're constantly striving to get better and better at it. Doing what you love to do and getting better at it is one of the greatest sources of happiness that there are. Being able to provide for yourself and your family, being financially independent, are very important.

One final thing with regard to success and happiness: you do outgrow other people in your family. My wife came from a poor family with ten children. They never had any money at all, and my wife now lives in a big house and has a wonderful life. Some of her brothers and sisters have been very snide, sneering, critical, demeaning of her because she has been so successful—not all of them, but some of them.

You may also find this happens with friends. You'll find that as you grow and develop yourself, and become more successful, you may find you have less and less in common with other people—the people you went to school with, the people you hung out with when you started your career. They're still watching TV and relieving tension and having a good time, and this is no longer your worldview. Sometimes you even have less and less in common with your spouse.

Your worldview is that you like to be productive. You like to be producing something. You like to be getting results, because it makes you happy and it opens up all kinds of opportunities and possibilities for you.

Dan

Brian, to wrap up, what are some takeaways for aligning money and happiness for those who have mastered the Science of Money?

Brian

The most important thing that I teach people—and I've practiced it myself all my life— is to imagine you could wave a magic wand over your life in four areas and make your life perfect in every way. What would it look like, and how would it be different from today, and what would be the first step that you could take to achieve that future dream?

The first area has to do with your income, your business, your career. If you were earning the kind of money you wanted to earn, doing the kind of work you love to do, with the kind of people that you enjoy, selling a product that you believe in to customers that you like—if your life were perfect in these ways, what would it look like, and how would it be different from today? What's the first step that you could take to begin moving from where you are today to that perfect future?

The second area has to do with your family and your relationships. If your relationships, family, lifestyle, home, vacations, everything, were just beautiful, how would they be different from today?

Third, look at your health: if your health was perfect, if you were absolutely supremely healthy, fit, lean, trim, the best you could possibly be, how would that be different from today, and what would be the first step you could take to move toward that goal?

Finally, your financial situation, which is financial freedom. Can you determine exactly how much money that you would need coming in each month from your investments to be able to retire and never have to work or worry about money again? How much money would that be? What would be that number? Set down that number as a goal, and project forward to when you would want to have it. Then go back to the present and ask, what would be the first thing you would have to do to start accumulating to that magic number where you would never have to work again?

Now here's the interesting discovery. People who do this do not think about not working again, because they want to continue working all their lives. They just want to have the choice. They want to be able to choose not to work. So pick your number.

Do you know that 80–90% of Americans don't know what that number is? Sit down and analyze your total expenses per month, both fixed and variable expenses, things that happen. Look at your bills. Look at your payments. How much would it cost you to live if you had no income coming in? That's the magic number. How much would it cost per month, per year?

Then you multiply that annual number by twenty. So if it costs you $5000 a month, that's $60,000 a year. That's $1.2 million. At that rate, you could draw down $5000 a month for twenty years, and you'll never run out of money for the rest of your life. If you need more, then calculate it out. Work it out. Write it down, and start striving toward that number today.

The very act of being clear about what your perfect life would look like in those four areas, and then taking the first step and starting to move toward it, will make you happy all the time.

TEN

The Science of Economics: Rules for a Vibrant National Economy

Before we conclude, let's elevate our viewpoint from the ground level of our own lives to the 50,000-foot level and see how what we have learned relates to our national and increasingly global economy as a whole. It's no secret that we face some difficult financial challenges in the United States, both now and in the near future. Brian believes that it is crucial, even our duty as responsible citizens, to know what it takes to make our economy thrive for decades to come. Then Brian will conclude with a review of what you've learned and how to make your *personal* economy one that thrives for years to come.

Dan

Brian, let's begin by having you discuss why you believe that understanding the basic rules of economics, not just on a personal level, but on a national level, is vitally important for every productive citizen in this nation.

Brian

I was confused about economics when I was growing up, and if you're confused, then you're very easily manipulated and moved by political rhetoric and demagoguery. In fact most of modern politics depends upon the economic ignorance of the populace.

There's a great story. There was a king, and he became very wealthy. He decided that he would collect all the wisdom of the world. That would be his legacy to the world, so he sent out his wise men all over the world with unlimited budgets to bring back the collective wisdom of mankind. And they came back with 100,000 books, and by this time he's about fifty or fifty-five years old. "That's too many books," he said. "You've got consolidate it down."

The wise men got together and consolidated and finally came up with 1000 books, but by this time he was sixty years old. He said, "I can never read 1000 books, so you've got to consolidate them down." So they went away and worked for another ten years, and they condensed the knowledge down to 100 books. Now he was in his seventies, and he was creaking. He said, "It's still too much. Can't you possibly summarize it even better?"

So they went away, and about five years later they came back to meet with the king. The leader of the wise men had one little piece of paper in his hand. He said, "We've been able to summarize all the wisdom of all the ages into one piece of paper, and here it is." He opened it up, and it said, "There ain't no free lunch."

This is the great principle of economics: there ain't no free lunch. In the Western world today we have what I call Santa Claus economics, something-for-nothing economics. Politicians use the public purse to buy themselves into office, and then they raise taxes to use the public purse to keep themselves in office. All of politics today is log rolling. You vote for my expenditure and my taxation, then I'll vote for yours. One hand scratches the other person's back, and so on. All politicians get into office by promising to give free money to other people—Santa Claus. Just watch: every election somebody is running as Santa Claus.

Every so often an adult stands up and says, "Where's the money going to come from?" They boo this person down. "The government will pay." But the rule in economics is that governments have no money. As Rush Limbaugh used to say, "It's not their money, folks." They have no money, except the money that they extract from the private sector.

Here's a very good picture. Imagine a swimming pool. A government employee takes a bucket and dips it in one end of the pool and runs around to the other end of the pool and pours it back in. That is exactly what governments do. They take money out of one end, from one person or group in one particular way, and then they go and they pour it back in, but there's no net gain in the economy.

But here's the worst thing. Because government servants are sloppy, they spill 80% of the water, so that the amount of water that actually gets poured back in is substantially less than they picked up in the first place. So as government expenditures go up, government or national wealth goes down. Unemployment goes up as government expenditures go up. Wages flatten out as government expenditures go up, because government is basically a dead weight on the society. Government produces nothing of value that people want, because if people wanted it, the private sector would produce it.

The mayor of Indianapolis had a way of transforming what was basically a debt-ridden economy. He called it the Yellow Pages test. He said, "If there is any function that the government performs for which there are three or more companies that perform it in the private sector, it's going to be farmed out." The public sector unions went hysterical, because they are paid extremely well. They're bankrupting virtually every city, state, and county and national government in the country with trillions of dollars of unfunded liabilities. They went hysterical. But he stuck to it.

So if you needed trash hauling, if you needed fire hydrant maintenance, if you needed gardening for municipal functions, parks, and things like that, if there was a company that did it, he put it out to bid. Surprisingly, the government unions came back. They had to bid in competition with the private sector, and their prices went down. The government unions began to lay off their own lazy people and began to do the jobs and do them well and do them at competitive prices.

Many years ago Henry Hazlitt, an economist, wrote a treatise called *Economics in One Lesson*, based on Frederic Bastiat's essay *What Is Seen and What Is Not Seen*. He said what you see is the result of government expenditure. Governments hire employees. What you don't see is that for every person that the government hires, two people must lose jobs in the private sector. You see that the government has created all of these new jobs, but you don't see the jobs that disappeared because businesspeople either laid people off or didn't start businesses in the first place, because their taxes were too high. These are all standard economic principles.

I remember a politician who was confronted with this question: "Do you know anything about basic economics? You can't take out what you don't put in. You can't consume what you don't produce. There ain't no free lunch." He said, "I know nothing about economics, and I don't want to know anything about economics, because if I did, it would change the way I voted." This is the disease that we have throughout the Western world.

We are seeing that Japan has tipped into recession. One of the most potentially prosperous economies, it was number three worldwide two decades ago, but then they brought in all these government taxation, regulation, and expenditure programs and strangled what was the third most prosperous country in the world. And this is happening now in France. France is dying.

In the U.S. today, more companies are dying than are being formed for the first time in American history. It used to be that more and more new companies were formed, and a certain number would die through attrition each year. Today it's reversed.

Actually our entrepreneurial and corporate sectors are dying out. Companies today are not expanding; they're leaving their money overseas, or they're leaving their money in the bank. Apple has $200 billion. They sit on it because it's not safe to invest it, because the government will take it away from you with regulations, taxation, new laws, so basically they have a whole team of lawyers and accountants protecting their money from the government. People are not willing to take risks.

That's our problem in economics today. The Santa Claus politicians are offering something for nothing—money that people have not earned and do not deserve—and they're buying votes with it. And every time they buy a vote, the next election they have to up the ante and offer even more or the public, which is very fickle, will just switch its vote to someone else who offers them more.

Dan

Right now our national debt is at unprecedented and unsustainable levels. Discuss how this debt bomb is taking the disease of something for nothing to a national level. Talk about this challenge that we face, how it occurred, what can be done to fix it, and what we can do as citizens to face this.

Brian

The debt is money that is borrowed. It's borrowed from the public in the form of government bonds, but ultimately it has to be paid back. The people who know nothing about economics say, "We owe it to ourselves, so we don't really owe it." Yes, we do.

Today we have zero interest rates. If our interest rates were running at 4% or 5% on a government debt of $18 trillion, 4% or 5% would work out to about a trillion dollars a year in interest. The country would go bankrupt. That's why they are fighting desperately to keep interest rates as close to zero as possible until they get out of office.

You'll notice that for people who work in the private sector and have pensions, the pensions are tied to the stock market. People who work in the government have pensions as well, but the pensions are not tied to anything. They're guaranteed unconditionally for life, and they are altered on the basis of inflation. So if the economy goes to hell in a handbasket, the politicians will end up with golden parachutes, fabulous pension benefits, and medical benefits that will be adjusted upward, so that they'll always be earning more money than when they left office.

A politician who serves two terms in Washington, will retire, I believe, with more than a million dollars in pension benefits. Plus they'll have a Cadillac medical plan for life. Where's the money going to come from? They don't want to talk about it.

There's an expression from Charles de Gaulle when he was talking about after he left office, that France would have chaos. He said, "Après moi, le déluge," which means, "After me, the deluge (flood)." That is, it'll all be over. "Fifty years after I leave office, all these chickens will come home to roost, all the bills will be payable, but I'll be gone. I'll be retired. I'll be sitting with my own private retirement plan with all my bills paid off with fabulous medical benefits, and the economy can go down the drain, but it won't affect my income because my income is completely separate from any other pension program. My income is guaranteed for as long as I live."

So we do have a lot of challenges. But here's what's worse. According to *Business Week*, the amount of unfunded liabilities, the amount that we owe not just in the national debt—$19.2 trillion—but in Social Security, Medicare, pensions, everything else that is unfunded, that means it's on the books, it has to be paid each year, is closer to $107 trillion. One hundred seven trillion dollars is about six times what the country earns in a year, and this means it can never be paid off. We are the most affluent country in history, and we owe so much debt it's crushing.

Estonia has very little debt. Many countries have no debt at all, and we have more debt than all the other countries in the world put together. The only solution they think of is, increase the debt limit: borrow more money that will never be paid back.

Dan

There's an old saying: if I owe $3000, I have a problem, but if I owe $3 million, the bank has a problem. The meaning behind that is, if I don't pay that money back, the bank somehow has to make it up, so they're going to do everything they can, especially if I have a massive loan with that bank, to make sure that I'm creditworthy and that I can pay it back. And so I wonder, is there any escape hatch in this scenario of the United States getting out from under this debt bubble, whereby other nations, such as China, would simply forgive the debt because of their reliance on us, particularly our consumers? Or is bankruptcy going to be our only way out of this situation?

Brian

They say because the U.S. dollar is the reserve currency, we can continue to print money and other people will hold it. The only thing we have going for us now is that almost every other country is politically more unstable. That's why more and more money comes to the U.S., because it's safer here. It's protected by law, so I think they will continue to punt it for a long time. They will pay it down, but what's coming down the bend are higher interest rates. Higher interest rates on this amount of debt are going to consume, first, all the discretionary spending available to the federal government. It's going to wipe out the entire defense budget, take out all of health, education, and welfare, eliminate Medicaid, unless they raise taxes by hundreds of billions and maybe even another trillion dollars and they have no choice.

If the interest rates go up, you have to pay 5% interest on this $18 trillion worth of deficit, but there are all those other deficits that have to be paid—Medicare and Social Security. They're all going broke. There's no trust fund. There's no saving. There are completely unfunded liabilities. There's not a penny put aside for any of this more than $100 trillion worth of debt. We owe more than all the countries in the world put together only because we can print dollars.

Dan

It's another reason why people need to listen and to apply all the lessons you are teaching. The generations coming up could face a reduced standard of living, and they will perhaps have to provide for themselves even more than previous generations. Discuss the book *Democracy in America* by Alexis de Tocqueville, the lessons it taught about why America was so successful in the early days, and how it points to areas where we may have fallen short in more recent years.

Brian

The primary message that I recall from Alexis de Tocqueville, who published his book in 1835, is that America was made up of individualists, people who accepted individual responsibility for their own work and for the results of their production. It was also made up of communitarians in that people cooperated together, with barn raisings, bringing in the crops, and so on.

He said that this was the most remarkable thing: There is no elite in America. There's no landed aristocracy. America was set up so that average people could come here and start with nothing, and by hard work and dint of entrepreneurial activity could create a wonderful life for themselves. De Tocqueville saw all this. He saw that the government at that time was extremely small, whereas the governments in Europe were enormous, overwhelming, oppressive. It led to revolutions and mass murders. There were revolutions in France, Germany, and Italy. There were eventually revolutions in Russia, where the working class rose up because of the taxes and oppression.

We never had that in the U.S. The U.S. was set up as anti-aristocratic. Nobody was better because they came from a wealthy family. One of the examples I like to use is Bill Gates, the richest man in America, as of this month worth $79 billion. Imagine that Bill Gates came up to you and said, "I'm Bill Gates and I'm the richest man in the America. Here, kiss my ring." Imagine if he'd said that to an immigrant, a poor person, a street person, an average person, a dishwasher. There's nobody in America who would kiss the ring of a person just because he's the richest man in the world. Americans would consider that to be ridiculous. We just don't do that.

But we're losing this sense of individuality and independence, and this is the great challenge. More and more people are becoming dependent upon the government and saying, "Why doesn't the government do this?"

I'll tell you a quick story. Alabama is very famous for having boars. These boars were vicious creatures. They were out in the woods, and nobody went out there because the boars would kill dogs, and they'd kill hunters.

One day this farmer drives into this area and stops at a little town. He said, "I want to catch me some of them boars." They said, "No, you don't want to go near those boars. If we go hunting with boars, we have dogs and we have rifles, because they are so dangerous." He said, "Just tell me where they are and leave it to me."

So they said, "You'll find them down there at the south end of the swamp." So he goes out, and he's gone for a few days. When he comes back, here's this big pickup, loaded with boars. They're all alive, and they're all oinking and jammed into this pickup shoulder to shoulder. He stops to get some gas. They ask, "How did you get them? Nobody could capture even one of those boars. They're the most vicious animals in the southern United States."

He said, "It was real easy. I took some cornmeal and I just put it on the ground and went away. The boars came out and sniffed around and finally ate the meal. And then I came back, and I did it again. I did it again the second day, and they came out. Then I started to build a little corral, about ten feet away, started to put some trees and some sticks down there. They came in and ate the meal and went away.

"I just kept building up this corral, and after a few days, they were coming there and lining up, getting ready for their free food. And they came up, and they ate the food." Then he closed the back of the corral, and the only place that the boars could go was out the other end, and the other end was the ramp up to the truck.

He put a trail of cornmeal right up into the back of the pickup. The boars walked up and got into the back. They jammed in all the way to the end and ate the meal. He closed the back of the pickup truck and drove away. He said, "It's easy. You make people dependent for any period of time, and they lose all sense of individuality, all sense of independence, all sense of danger. They become meek and mild and easily controlled."

This has been the policy of governments throughout the world, to make people meek and controlled by giving them free things until finally they become too weak to resist. That's what we're doing, not only here but throughout the world. Most government policies are designed to make people completely dependent on the government so that they will vote for the government, which promises to keep the gravy train coming.

Dan

Brian, in a nonpartisan way, can we discuss some specifics of the science of economics and how each area makes a difference in how effectively an economy works? Here are some topics for our discussion: tax policy, minimum wage laws, regulations, size of government, such as federal versus state, and any other areas that you feel are important to a proper understanding of basic economics.

Brian

The bottom line is that everything government does it makes worse, because everything that goes through government is political. That means it is controlled by a political agenda. And the political agenda is always to enrich your friends and punish your enemies. That's why every single political contribution is a quid pro quo. I contribute my money, but I expect a big payoff from the politicians if they get into office. You're gambling, putting your money on that horse. If that horse wins, that horse is going to pay you off. It's going to give you a good ride.

There is an organization in Washington that analyzes the amount of campaign contribution versus the amount of government benefits that company gets in the next four years. Today it's running 72 to 1. There was a solar panel company that went bankrupt. The founder of the company gave $100,000 to Obama in the first election. He got $526 million back from the government in the next two years, even though in the government they said, "This is a complete waste of time, this company has no products, it has no ability to ever pay the money back." That's the biggest payoff that I know of. The money disappeared, and to this day nobody has asked where it went. They were told from the White House, "Just give them the money," because they were trying to send a signal to other donors. It worked, because they raised $800 million in the next election. Everybody knew the big payoffs.

What we know is that as government grows, the private sector declines. The private sector produces products and services that people want and need and are willing to pay for—products and services that are considered to be actual wealth, for example cars, clothes, homes, furniture, cell phones. This is what people consider to be wealth, because it enhances their standard of living.

Government expenditures on hundreds of thousands and millions of employees who sit around most of the day do not create wealth. Some say that GNP grows when we hire more government servants. No, because you have to kill two jobs in the private sector to hire one person to work for the government, and then these people sit around most of the time. *Hard work* and *government employee* never appear in the same sentence. They would laugh at you.

The fact is that as government grows, the hopes and possibilities for the people decline, and so they have found over and over again that the only way to increase real genuine prosperity and opportunity is to decrease the size of government, decrease regulations, decrease taxes; let the people go. Leave the people to be free; get out of their way.

Most businesspeople in America says, "Just get out of the way. We don't want any government help. We don't want any policies. We don't want anything. Just leave us alone and let us build and operate our businesses." You'll find that the economies around the world that are booming are the ones that have the least regulation and the lowest taxes. The ones that are dying are the ones that have the most regulations and the highest taxes, and this is true right across the spectrum. America used to be the freest nation in the world. It's now number nineteen. It's just below Botswana.

In his book *Trust: The Social Virtues and the Creation of Prosperity*, Francis Fukuyama, the historian, showed that the economies that had the highest levels of trust were also the most prosperous. The economies that had the lowest level of trust were the most impoverished. They have done indices on ease of doing business as well. The economies where it's the easiest to start a business are the most prosperous; those where it's the most difficult to do business are the least prosperous. Transparency International also says the countries that have the most corruption are the least prosperous, those with the least corruption are the most prosperous.

For several decades after World War II, the U.S. led all these indices. Now the U.S. is running number nineteen. It's even running number eighteen or nineteen in terms of educational attainment. We spend more per student than any other country in the world, and we have the worst outcomes. So until you have leadership that can stand up and say, "This is not good, we have to reverse it, we've got to start making it easier for people to work and start businesses, we've got make it easier for people to do business and to trade nationally and internationally"—until we do that, there's no government policy that can possibly help.

Dan

There's been a great deal of discussion recently about the top 1% versus the 99%. Many people believe that capitalism is at a cancerous stage, where the rich keep getting richer and everyone else will continue to stay the same or get poorer. Statistics that show flat wages for the vast majority of the country, with huge increases in wealth for the very top, particularly the top 0.1%, suggest that these concerns may be valid. Discuss your feelings about this controversy. Is it a valid concern? Do you think capitalism can still work effectively at this stage in our economy?

Brian

As I said before, capitalism is actually savings-ism. If you could imagine a primitive farmer who plants a seed and brings in the harvest, what does he do with the crop? He puts seed aside for planting the next year, and that seed is taken away from the amount of food that he and his family can consume. In other words, he deprives himself and others. He saves his money. He sacrifices. He practices delayed gratification. Throughout all of human history these have been the qualities of success.

In the same way, if you work hard and you earn money and you take some of that money and save it, and then you invest that money carefully in something like an income-producing piece of real estate, or a stock or bond or a mutual fund, or something that generates revenue, then what you are doing is you are becoming a capitalist, which means a savings-ist. The word *capitalist* came from Karl Marx, who did not understand cause and effect. He just saw wealthy people, but wealthy people save their money, and they reinvest it. There's an enormous amount of risk, and very high levels of failure. And sometimes there are long periods of time before there's a return.

If you build a factory, the factory may cost you three to five years to build and three to five years to make a profit, so a person has to be willing to invest for a ten-year period before it starts to make money. And then the Pikettys and the Stiglitzes and the socialists go around and say, "Look at this wealthy son of a gun, making all this money from manufacturing these products, marking the products up two, three, four, five times and ripping off the poor consumer." What about the ten years that that person invested to build the factory or the business in the first place? A small business takes seven years to reach profitability. The day it reaches profitability, the tax people are in, and they want 50% of your profits, because they have no understanding of cause and effect.

So the problem we have in America with inequality is that people don't save their money. They're taught to spend their money, to spend it on fun, to buy big televisions, go to Las Vegas. Every state now has legalized gambling, so if you can't go to Las Vegas, you can gamble right where you are. The fact is that if you save your money and invest it carefully, eventually you become a capitalist. You're a savings-ist. Where there are no savings, there is no capital accumulation, then there's no future for the nation.

But savings means you have to deprive yourself of the joy of consumption today in order to enjoy a higher level of consumption sometime in the future. Savings means putting off into the future the consumption that you could enjoy today. It is only the willingness of people to do that that makes a civilized society possible. Countries where there's no security or safety for savings, corrupt countries, dishonest countries, are countries where people don't save.

The reason the U.S. is such a safe place to invest is that money is carefully protected by law. You cannot steal money without going to jail. In other places you can steal with both hands and live in a palace on the hill, and you can buy off all the politicians and the judges and the courts, which is what is causing these countries to be in such terrible shape, because nobody wants their money.

The fact is that you cannot consume what you don't produce. The job of government is to create an environment where the natural, spontaneous entrepreneurial instinct of individuals will lead to the development of new products and services and businesses. And they'll hire people and create jobs and opportunities, and they'll pay more taxes, which pay for all the schools and hospitals and universities and roads and everything else. That's basic economics, and we are living in cloud-cuckoo-land. We're thinking that it's possible for government to continue to strangle the private sector and that's it's not going to have any long-term effect. And they all expect to be out of office and living on fat pensions before the chickens come home to roost.

With regard to income inequality, everybody is born unequal, and here's the great problem. I've studied and written about this extensively. Most people are unequal by choice. They're unequal in that they stopped upgrading their knowledge and skills decades ago. They had bad influences or no influences. They did poorly in school, for whatever reason. They came out illiterate.

Fifty percent or more of high school students in America graduate illiterate and are unable to fill out an application form to work at McDonald's. Fifty to sixty percent of university students who are being admitted have to take remedial courses on English and math during the summer in order to be able to take basic 101-level courses in the fall. These people have no skills. They can't read. They can't operate computers. They don't understand science or mathematics or engineering. They have no knowledge of business or management or marketing. They have no way to create value. They have no earning ability, and as a result their incomes are lower.

As Gary Becker of the University of Chicago said, we don't have an income gap; we have a skills gap. The people in the bottom 80% have not improved their skills for decades. They came out, worked for one year, and never read a book. The people in the top 20% are always upgrading their skills and increasing their value, so the inequality is self-inflicted. Each person decides to be equal or unequal in a good or bad way by whether or not they work on themselves and increase their ability to contribute value to their fellow man.

When a person says, "I've been working at McDonald's for ten years. I'm thirty-five years old. I'm getting $8 an hour, and I've got seven children with no husband at home," then whose fault is that? Who made all of those lifestyle choices that gets a person to that situation? At a certain point someone has to say that individuals are largely responsible for their own lives. As soon as you take away the idea of responsibility, the society falls apart. Actually the society only stays together because so many people *do* accept high levels of responsibility and don't blame their problems on other people.

Dan

Another economic concern is the effect of automation, not just now, but in the future, and how it may flatten wages and impact jobs. What does this portend for the future of employment in America? Do you think more people should consider going the entrepreneurial route as a result?

Brian

There have been waves of automation since 1770. Every single time that there was a wave of automation, new factories, spinning wheels, there was a huge outcry—this is going to destroy jobs and leave people in the streets. In every single case what automation does is to systematize simple, boring jobs, and it frees people up to do higher-order work that is more enjoyable and more challenging. Therefore each time automation comes in, it actually creates more jobs.

When the automobile came out, the practice was to manufacture cars using teams, so an automobile plant may have had twenty or thirty teams, and each would be working on a car. When industry came up with the production line, automation, and scientific management, they were able to hire hundreds and thousands of people. Hundreds of car factories grew up to employ tens of thousands and millions of people at higher standards of living, with better wages, better health care.

For the first time in history a man could afford to work, and his whole family could stay at home. Up until that time the whole family had to work, the kids begging, the mothers working in the fields, the father working at a crummy job. But with automation, suddenly one man could provide for his whole family, and his kids could go to school and his wife could stay home.

The challenge is that with automation you have to upgrade your skills, and you have to continue upgrading your skills all your life. Every single time a job is automated, it frees people up to do higher-level work, and that is one of the blessings. If it wasn't for automation, we'd all still be living on the farm.

Do you know that at the turn of the twentieth century, 50% of Americans lived on the farm, feeding the other 50%? Today less than 1% of Americans live on the farm, and they feed 330 million people, and they export shiploads of surplus food all over the world to rich and poor countries—because of automation. So automation is a great thing, but it requires that you upgrade your skills.

Dan

Brian, as we are coming to the end, I thought it would be good if you could give us a review, call it a minicourse, on the economic laws and principles that make for a vibrant national economy. Can you share that with us?

Brian

Yes. I culled these economic laws from my years and years of research. In mathematics, there are certain principles that, once understood, enable the mathematician to solve complex problems that would be impossible for the average person. In mechanics, there are certain proven principles that enable a skilled craftsman to repair an automobile or an airplane using certain methods, processes, and tools that would be difficult for an untrained average person. In economics, there are certain laws that explain all of human behavior and which are essential for the entrepreneur to understand.

The first is the *law of scarcity*. It's the fundamental law of economics. It says economic goods have value because the supply of them available is less than the amount that is desired. In other words, there are never enough houses. There are never enough cars. There are never enough diamond rings or beautiful watches or extra clothes. Scarcity is what gives value to everything. This idea that there should be a surplus, that everybody should be able to have all they want of some good, guaranteed by government, is nonsense. There will always be scarcity.

In terms of economics, you must continually choose among various options, because you cannot have everything you want. Only little children stomp their feet and scream and have tantrums, saying, "I want this and I want that." The fact is that you always have to choose, because your ability to purchase things is always limited. And because goods are scarce, trade-offs are always necessary. This is the great law of economics that governs societies: you cannot give everything to everyone at all times under all conditions. There just isn't enough.

The second law is the *law of supply and demand*. This says that the price of a good or service is in direct proportion to the available supply relative to the demand at the point of acquisition. The wage, for example, of a fast-food worker, the price of that fast-food worker, which is basically a commodity, is determined by how many people are willing to work at fast-food places for minimum wage. The fact is that because people have no other skills, they are willing to work by the millions at those places.

If somebody says, "I won't work for less than $15 an hour," they will be replaced in about five minutes by a whole list of people who line up to get jobs at that place for $8 or $7.75 an hour, because of supply and demand. There's no objective price. It's always based on how much people want something and how much they are willing to pay.

This law of supply and demand determines all prices, all profits, all wages, all growth, decline, costs, losses, and the success or failure of every business. It's the same with any company that exports. It's always supply and demand. Successful entrepreneurs work continually to increase the demand for what they are selling so that they can increase the price they charge. This is what all of advertising, marketing, and promotion is aimed at increasing the demand.

Another principle is that entrepreneurs continually seek to provide their products and services better, cheaper, faster, or more conveniently so that they can increase the demand for them. That's the basic law. The law of scarcity: everything is scarce; the law of supply and demand: price is determined by how much people want it. As we said before, the number one reason companies go broke is that nobody wants the product at that price.

The *law of substitution* in economics says certain goods and services can be substituted for each other when the supply and demand ratio for them changes. I'll give you an example. When beef becomes too expensive, people substitute and buy chicken. When gasoline prices become too high, people buy smaller cars. When labor prices become too high, companies automate and replace workers with machines. It's always a cost-benefit relationship. If I can pay for this machine and by saving these wages, I can earn more in the long run, then that's a good investment.

Customers always have three choices in the marketplace: they can buy the product or service offered, or they can buy something from some other company, your competitor, or they can refrain from buying anything at all. Whenever you go into the marketplace, your customer always has those three choices: buy from you, buy from a competitor, or not buy anything at all. This is the *law of substitution.*

The *law of connectivity* is another great economic law. It says various products and services are connected to each other in either a positive or a negative way and directly or inversely affect the price of each other. For example, when the price of an item goes up, it often causes the price of something connected to it to go up as well. Food price increases lead to restaurant price increases. That's why they're saying today here in San Diego that you can't get prime rib at the best restaurants because beef prices have gone up because corn prices have gone up. Prime rib prices have gone up, and it's too expensive to offer on the menu anymore. So why can't you get prime rib? It's because of the connectivity of all these prices.

When the price of an item goes up, it causes the demand for something else to go down. When restaurant prices go up, the number of people going to that restaurant can go down. Or you may have a reverse connectivity: the number of people going to fast-food restaurants may increase if the prices in expensive restaurants go up.

Everything is interwoven with everything else, so price connectivity can affect the cost of other products. If people stop going to a restaurant, the restaurant can end up buying fewer food products from other suppliers, so it can have a reverse domino effect. If a business stops selling more of its product, it cuts back on the raw materials, it cuts back on labor—again, connectivity.

There's a story about a guy who has just commissioned a painting from an artist because his business is doing very well. He goes into a restaurant, and he sits there. There's a poster on the wall. It's from a newspaper that says hard times are coming. The economy is about to drop. We're going to have recession, depression, and unemployment. He's looking at that, and he thinks, "Geez, I hadn't even thought about that. Here I've paid all this money for this painting."

So he goes to the phone, and he calls up and he cancels the commission. The artist had just called someone to come and paint her house, because she thought she had the money for that. Now she cancels the job. Then the housepainter calls the car dealer, because he had just gotten this painting job, and was going to get a new car. It goes like this all the way through the economy.

Well, the first guy goes back into the restaurant a couple of days later, and he looks at the poster. He looks a little closer, and he finds that the poster was put up and framed twenty-five years before.

The point is that the wrong piece of information can lead to a connectivity like this, which has a cascading negative effect. That's why whenever they pronounce that unemployment is up, the stock market drops. People sell their shares, they run for cover. Then they say, "Unemployment isn't that bad," and the shares all rush up again. The whole stock market is affected by news.

The next law is called the *law of marginality*. It says that all economic decisions, and therefore all prices and costs, are determined by the *last* purchase decision made. This is an important thing to understand. The amount that the *last* customer will pay for the *last* item available determines the price of the whole supply. Let's say you sell donuts, and the hungriest person, who wants donuts more than anything, will pay a dollar apiece for them because he wants them so badly. But you can't sell your donuts at a dollar apiece, because there'd only be a few people that would pay that amount. You have to sell your donuts at a much lower price so that more and more people can come into the market. And you keep charging it at a price that is low enough, but on which you can still make a profit, so that you can sell more and more.

Let's say you get the price down to $0.50 a donut or $0.25 a donut. Then everybody can have donuts—as long as you're making a profit at the last available sale. The principle of marginality says it's not that what one highly motivated customer will pay, it's what the last discriminating, careful, cautious customer will pay that sets the price for everything that you offer. It's always the last customer who can buy that product or buy it somewhere else that sets the price. If I can get it somewhere else at $0.25 and you're charging $0.26, I'll go to that other place. So the *market clearing price* is the price at which all customers will satisfy their needs and all sellers will sell their products and services.

If you go to a public market, you'll find that people bring their produce to sell. Their goal is to have an empty stand at the end of the day, so that the last customer buys the last product from the last stand and everybody goes home. Everything is sold. That is the market clearing price. What you do is, you price at the market clearing price for the *first* customer of the day so that by the end of the day everything has been sold. This principle of marginality is essential to all pricing.

The next law is called the *law of decreasing returns*, which is important both personally and in business. It says the returns, rewards, or profits from some economic activities decrease over time. It says you can often earn high profits from the first products or services you sell. The cost of producing those products or services, however, can increase, and later you could earn fewer profits on the product or service, because your costs have become much higher. There are many activities that you engage in that have a decreasing value. The more of them you do, the less value they have to your customers.

Then there is *the law of increasing returns*. The profitability of a product, service, or activity can increase as you produce or offer more of it. This, by the way, is the reason for the success of mass manufacturers. In the retail sector, Walmart, for example, increases their returns because they buy more and more products, hundreds of thousands, millions, and spread them over 11,000 stores. They get the prices so low that they become the first-choice source for all of these products for millions and millions of customers every day.

Knowledge is the real source of competitive advantage today. As you produce a knowledge-based product, you become more efficient with every additional unit. It therefore costs you less to produce each unit, increasing the profits you earn on each unit you sell.

I'll give you an example of increasing returns. I do a wonderful seminar called Twenty-First Century Selling. For me to produce that seminar, it took hundreds of hours of research and years of experience on the Street. Once I gave the seminar and polished it using feedback. I now have a seminar that is one of the best one-day seminars on selling in the world. I've given that seminar over 300 times all over the world and charge my fees, which are quite high. If someone says, "We need a sales seminar," I can start in five minutes, because I've paid an enormous price to develop that intellectual product. Once it's produced, it can be reproduced at a very low price. So knowledge-based products have the benefit of increasing returns. The more of them you sell, the more profitable they are.

The next law—and this is really important to our discussion about international and national economics—is called *the law of secondary consequences*. It says that every action has both primary and secondary consequences. For everything that you do, something else happens as a result, and for many things that you fail to do, there's a consequence as well.

According to the economists, Bastiet and Hazlitt and others, the primary consequence is always positive. A person says, "I'm going to drop out of school and get a job and get a car and have girls." The primary consequence is positive. He's cool, he's got a car, he's got girlfriends. What are the secondary consequences? Lack of education, a low-level job, high levels of unemployment throughout his life, no skills in automation. Eventually he's poor. This is one of the great problems in our world today: an enormous number of people engage in activities that have very serious secondary consequences.

Economist Milton Friedman said that the ability to accurately consider what's likely to happen as a secondary consequence is the key to excellent thinking. It's not the *primary* consequence, which is always something advantageous. You eat a box of donuts. I've seen people eat a box of Krispy Kreme donuts. The primary result is the deliciousness of the donuts, but the secondary result is that you're going to feel sluggish. You're not going to sleep very well. If you keep doing this over time, you're going to get overweight. You're going to have a big gut. You're going to have to buy clothes that are larger, and so on. So the secondary consequences of what seemed to be a nice thing to do can be tremendous, or they can be awful.

The next law is called *the law of unintended consequences*. The ultimate consequences of many actions are far worse than if nothing had been done at all. This explains almost all government policies. Sometimes an action taken to generate profits actually generates losses. This is a great danger in business. We can go all-in on an investment and end up being broke or losing all our money and being far worse off than if we hadn't made the investment at all. Unintended consequences always occur when any action depends for its success on violating the principle of expediency, which I'll explain in a couple of minutes, the something-for-nothing Santa Claus mentality.

The next law, *the law of choice*, says that every human action entails a choice among alternatives, and the choice is always based on the dominant values of the individual at that moment. Your true values are always expressed in your actions. You can always tell what a person thinks, believes, and values by looking at what they do, not at what they say or wish or hope.

If you have two types of donuts on the table, you'll always choose the donut that you want more. If you have two people to marry, you'll choose the one you value the most. It's the same when you have two cars to buy, two jobs to take, two courses to enroll in. By your action, you'll always prove what is most valuable and important to you.

This was a shocker to me, because it finally explained why people would say one thing and do something else and then they would explain it away—everybody does it, or it doesn't matter. They would say this, and you think, "Wait a minute. No, what you do is a true expression of who you fundamentally are, so every action you take, or decline to take, implies a choice and a statement about your values and beliefs." Once I understood that, I understood the world.

The next law is the *law of the excluded alternative*, which says whatever you choose to do, you're simultaneously excluding all other choices at that moment. Every choice implies a rejection of all other choices, at least for the moment, especially in the marketplace. When you have a choice, you have scarcity and limited supply. When you have a choice, you always choose what is most important to you, but in choosing, you reject all other possible choices. When you marry one person, you reject all other people that you could marry in the whole world, or at least you had better. And every choice that you make tells yourself and others what you truly believe and value.

The last law—and this is the basis of the entire Austrian school—is *the law of subjective value*. The value of anything is subjective. It is determined by what someone is willing to pay for it, and this explains inequality and why people's incomes are flat and so on. You cannot tell anybody what your job is worth. It's worth what someone else is willing to pay you freely in a free economy when they can choose someone else. And this is a shock. All attempts to get above-market rates must use government force, legislation, punishment, fines, and everything else.

We had a major meltdown in 2008–2009. It was caused because the federal government passed laws that made it mandatory for the banks to lend to people who had no credit, because the politicians hoped that these people would then vote for them in the next election. It started under Jimmy Carter. It was expanded under Bill Clinton, and it rolled on like Old Man River under George W.

Bush. People were actually being given money to buy houses. They were getting credit back. They were buying houses with 3% down, and they would get a 3% bonus once they moved into the house. The banks funded tens of thousands, hundreds of thousands, several million homes that people could not afford, and it all came crashing down. It was 100% government endorsed. They said that these homes have a value in and of themselves, when the value was only created by giving people the money to buy them.

All prices set by individuals or businesses are educated guesses about how much people will pay to consume the entire supply produced. This brings us to the idea that all sales of merchandise or services at reduced prices are admissions by the vendors that the initial asking price was too high. They guessed wrong.

Only the person being asked to pay for a product or service is capable of determining what the product or service is worth. And in a free society, as Milton Friedman said, every single choice is a free choice. We make the choice because we feel that we will be better off as a result. If government interferes, then it destroys the opportunity for free choice.

The *law of maximization*, the final law that explains all economic activity, is that every person seeks to maximize his or her situation in every action to get the very most for the very least. This is also called the *principle of expediency*. It says that human beings are greedy, lazy, impatient, ambitious, selfish, ignorant, and vain, and they constantly strive for survival, security, comfort, leisure, love, respect, and fulfillment. This principle goes on to say that people inevitably seek the fastest and easiest way to get the things they want right now, with little concern for secondary consequences.

All economic activity is built around these principles. All economic results can be explained by reference to these laws, which state that people always strive to get the most for the least, with little or no concern for secondary or unintended consequences, and that expecting people *not* to act expediently is simply dreaming. It's like expecting people to change their eye color or expecting them not to breathe and still be healthy.

One example is welfare payments, which has helping the less fortunate as a primary consequence. But too much welfare, too long, and the secondary consequence is that people become dependent on government. They have no self-respect, no ability to work, no skills. Their income flattens out. They have no hope for themselves, for the future, for their children.

If everybody took advantage of these government programs and nobody worked, the society would collapse tomorrow. The only reason it doesn't is that we are hoping that a sufficient number of people will *not* take advantage of these programs, will *not* act expediently, will *not* take the fastest and easiest way to get the things they want with no concern for secondary consequences.

So that's my take on economics. There are many more laws, but the bottom line is, as I said at the beginning, there ain't no free lunch. If you apply that rigorously to all government policies and activities—and you have to apply them to the private sector—then governing would be completely different and much better for all of us and for the future.

Dan

Finally, Brian, let's conclude by discussing the impact that a life well lived, a life lived by implementing the laws outlined in this program, can have as a legacy for future generations.

Brian

No matter how many problems there are, there's a Greek saying, remember in times like these that there have always been times like these; that no matter how many problems we have in the world today, this is still the best time in all of human history to be alive. There are many things that are happening in our world politically and economically over which we have no control. What we do is to focus on what we *can* control. Throughout all of human history, success comes from those who become very good at what they do, and then they produce a very good product or service that people choose to buy in comparison with other similar products and services and buy again and again.

These people earn a very good living, and they save their money. As I said, capitalism is savings-ism. They save their money, and they invest it in resources that will continue to yield money long after the investment has been made. Eventually, over the course of your lifetime, you reach the point where your invested money is earning more than you are. At that point you can, if you want, gradually begin to back out of your profession or do it differently or do it in a different place. Some people go off and become missionaries and work in foreign countries.

Your job is to take 100% responsibility for your financial life and realize that it's totally under your control, and that wherever you are today, you can pay off your debts, save money, build a financial fortress, invest that money carefully into income-producing property, and achieve financial independence for yourself and your family. Sometimes it will happen far faster than you realize if you'll get started right away.

INDEX

A

abundance mentality, 147–149
accelerating acceleration, law of,
    164–165
accumulation, law of, 162–163
action and reaction, law of, 34
advice from experts, 83–84, 134, 160,
    174, 180
affirmations, 78
Affluent Society, The (Stanley), 193
Alice in Wonderland (Carroll), 33
allowances, 198
Amazon, 84
American Management Association,
    144
Amway, 71
Apple, 3–4, 164, 184, 207; iPhone, 137–
    141, 153; iPod, 17
Aristotle, 33
Army Corps of Engineers, 9
aspirations, 193
athletes, professional, 17, 22
attraction/magnetism, law of, 44–55,
    163–164
Austrian school of economics, 3, 231
Automatic Millionaire, The (Bach), 73

automation, 221–222
automobiles. *see* cars

B

Bach, David, 73
bank loans, 24–25, 51, 63
bankruptcy, 19, 90, 131–132, 138, 210,
    215
barter, 2
Baruch, Bernard, 169–171
basketball, 17, 22
Bastiat, Frederick, 206, 229
Becker, Gary, 112, 220
being needs, 194
belief, law of, 33
Berkshire Hathaway, 20
Bezos, Jeff, 84
Bible, 37, 45
Billings, Josh, 33
Blackberry, 137–138
Blakely, Sara, 149, 152–153
bootstrapping, 102–103
Buffett billionaires, 152
Buffett, Warren, 10–11, 20–21, 64, 75,
    76, 133, 143, 149, 151–152, 165, 171,
    188–189, 190

Bush, George W., 231–232
business failure rates, 43, 82, 88, 90
business forms, 183–186; C corporation, 184–186; LLC (limited liability company), 185; S corporation, 184, 185; sole proprietorship, 184, 185
business model reinvention, 35, 110
business models, 17, 35, 110, 140–143
business plans, 144–145
Business Week magazine, 209

C

capital gains taxes, 171
capitalism, 148–149, 217–220, 234
cargo cults, 8–9
Carrey, Jim, 52
cars: automobile insurance, 105, 180; extended car loans, 58, 63, 91, 106; manufacturing process, 57–58, 221–222; new *versus* used, 73–74
Carter, Jimmy, 231
cash: credit cards *versus*, 18–20, 86, 94–95; reserves, 26, 122, 128, 171, 183
cash flow, 27, 63, 76, 81–82, 132–133, 173–174, 182–183, 202
casinos, 10, 64–67, 189–190, 218
cause and effect, law of, 5, 33–43, 157–158, 218
C corporation, 184–186
children: allowances, 198; entrepreneurship of, 14, 151, 197–199; happiness and, 197–199
China: offshoring by Apple, 3–4; offshoring by IBM, 136; U.S. debt and, 210
Chobani, 127
choice, law of, 230–231
Citibank, 23
Clason, George, 94
Cleveland Clinic, 110–111
Clinton, Bill, 231
cocaine, 47
collateral, 25, 63, 87
Collins, Jim, 137

Columbia University, 151–152
Colvin, Geoffrey, 112
commodity trading, 23
competition, 29–30; competitive mind-set, 136–137; in investing, 133–134; in the workplace, 4
competitive advantage, 228–229
compliments, 41
compounding, law of, 12–13, 16, 30–31, 62, 160–162
connectivity, law of, 225–226
conservation, law of, 70–71
consignment sales, 102–103, 152
continuous and never-ending improvement (CANEI), 153–155
continuous improvement, 7–8, 11–13, 143, 153–155
correspondence, law of, 44–45
corruption, 216, 219
creative mind-set, 136–137
credit cards, 18–20, 91–93; cash purchases *versus*, 18–20, 86, 94–95; debt consolidation, 19–20, 73, 93–94; how to use, 91; special offers, 92
credit ratings, 25, 93
cross collateral, 25
crossover time, 62–63
customer cocreation, 138–140

D

Davis, Marvin, 159
days worked per week, 7–8
day trading, 10–11, 166
De Angelis, Barbara, 28
debt management, 85–107; bank loans, 24–25, 51, 63; bankruptcy, 19, 90, 131–132, 138, 210, 215; car loans, 58, 63, 91, 106; collateral, 25, 63, 87; credit card (*see* credit cards); debt consolidation, 19–20, 73, 93–94; documents concerning, 92, 106; eliminating debt, 80–81, 95; good and bad debt, 89–90; good faith payments, 87, 93–94; home equity line of credit,

91; interest-only payments, 87; line of credit, 25, 63, 87, 91; mortgages, 95–96, 106, 131–132, 231–232; national debt, 208–209; personal guaranty, 25, 132; snowball method to pay down, 99–101; starting a business, 24–25, 80–81, 86–90, 91, 100; student loans, 96–99

decreasing returns, law of, 227–228
deferred compensation plans, 60, 99, 208–209
"deficiency" needs, 194
de Gaulle, Charles, 209
delayed gratification, 99–101, 217–220
Democracy in America (Tocqueville), 211–212
depressions, 63
DeVos, Rich, 71
digital marketing, 154
disability insurance, 178–179, 180, 183
distortions in economy, 8
diversification, 170
dividends, 184
divine discontent, 189
dollar cost averaging, 166
Drucker, Peter, 6, 88, 143
Ducaisse, Alain, 113
due diligence, 27, 83, 158–160, 168, 170, 171, 173–174
Dun & Bradstreet, 120

E

earning ability: appreciating/depreciating, 15–16, 17–18; investing in increasing, 11–13, 20–21, 77–81, 96–99, 219–220, 222
earning years, 62–63
eBay, 84
economics, 203–234; Austrian school, 3, 231; laws of, 223–233; log rolling, 205; national debt, 208–209; Santa Claus (*see* something for nothing); taxes, 205–207, 216; unfunded liabilities, 209–211; Yellow Pages test, 206

Economics on One Lesson (Hazlitt), 206
educational attainment, 216–217, 219–220
E factor (expediency factor), 54–55, 232–233
Einstein, Albert, 16, 54, 160–161
Emerson, Ralph Waldo, 37
employees: earning ability, 15–16, 17–18, 20–21, 96–99; mind-set to become an entrepreneur, 128–130; preemptive pay increases, 23–24, 115–116; productivity of, 6–7, 114–115; steady income *versus* entrepreneurship, 192–193; survival bonus, 116–118; wealth creation methods, 60–62
end-of-life discussions, 182
entrepreneurship: business failure rates, 43, 82, 88, 90; business models, 17, 35, 110, 140–143; of children, 14, 151, 197–199; debt and, 24–25, 80–81, 86–90, 91, 100; demand for product or service, 124–128, 137–138; entrepreneurial ethic, 37, 63; franchising, 141–142, 145–147; income generation through, 119–125; income spikes, 193; inventory management, 90; job creation and, 219; mind-set shift, 128–130; network marketing, 102–103, 144–145; owner draw size, 125–126; sales and selling (*see* sales and selling); seven-year rule for profitability, 88–89, 125–126, 132–133, 145–146; stages of starting a business, 137–140; steady job *versus*, 192–193; system, 145–147
envy, 38–39, 43, 47, 188
Ericsson, K. Anders, 112
estate planning, 180–182
exchange. *see* law of exchange
excluded alternative, law of the, 231
executive compensation: golden parachutes, 8, 9–10, 208; severance pay, 9, 18, 128; signing bonuses, 18

expediency factor, 54–55, 232–233
experts, advice from, 83–84, 134, 160, 174, 180

F

Facebook, 31, 150, 154, 164
family. *see* relationships
family-limited trusts, 176–177
fear: of failure, 72–73; of sales and selling, 199–200
Festinger, Leon, 43, 188
Fidelity Magellan Fund, 60, 165
financial freedom/independence, 27–28, 157, 162, 164, 173. *see also* investing; saving; Financial Freedom account, 73, 94; law of correspondence, 45; magic wand exercise, 202; reticular activating system, 49–54
financial plans, 83
flash trading, 10–11, 166
Forbes magazine, 64, 88, 124, 159
forced savings, 177–178
force field of energy, 45–46
Ford, Henry, 57–58
Fortune 500, 9, 11, 16, 17
Fortune magazine, 16, 112
401(k) plans, 60, 99
France, 207, 209, 212
franchising, 141–142, 145–147
freedom, 27–28
French Laundry, The, 113
Friedman, Milton, 229, 232
frugality, 29–30, 57, 62, 64, 73–74, 81–82, 83–84
Fugger, Jacob, 29
Fukuyama, Francis, 216

G

gambling, 8, 10–11, 31, 64–67, 165–166, 189–190, 192, 218
Gates, Bill, 140–141, 142–143, 146, 212
Gerber, Michael, 145
Gerstner, Lou, 120–121
get-rich-quick schemes, 54–55, 60–61, 64–67, 109, 116–119, 189–190, 191, 204–207, 208–209
Gibran, Kahlil, 46
Gladwell, Malcolm, 112
goals, 143–145
golden age of mankind, 157
golden parachutes, 8, 9–10, 208
Good to Great (Collins), 137
Google, 17, 84, 98, 164
Graham, Ben, 151–152
Gray, Albert, 72
guaranteed investments, 165

H

hands-on management, 146–148
happiness, 42, 69, 187–202: challenges and roadblocks, 193–197; children and, 197–199; envy and resentment *versus*, 38–39, 43, 47, 188; magic wand exercise, 201–202; misconceptions, 190–193; money and, 187–190; resilience, 199–200; self-concept level of income, 192; social comparison theory, 43, 188–190
Harvard University, 30–31, 43, 98, 150, 188
Hay, Louise, 80
Hazlitt, Henry, 206, 229
health: law of correspondence, 44–45; magic wand exercise, 201; weight management, 44–45, 101, 103, 229–230
health insurance, 104, 208, 209
herd instinct, 72
hesitation, 72
Hewlett, Bill, 130
Hewlett-Packard, 130
Hill, Napoleon, 34, 39
homes: as collateral, 25, 63; decision to buy, 52–53, 63–64, 75; home equity line of credit, 91; home insurance, 105; mortgages, 95–96, 106, 131–132, 231–232; rental, 87, 131–132
homo economicus, 3

hours worked, 6–7, 12, 47–48, 118, 195

HR magazine, 78

Hussein, Saddam, 55

I

IBM, 120–121, 136, 142–143

Inc. magazine, 126

income generation, 108–134; advice of experts, 83–84, 134, 160, 174, 180; get-rich-quick schemes, 54–55, 60–61, 64–67, 109, 116–119, 189–190, 191, 204–207, 208–209; income of associates, 39, 188–189; magic wand exercise, 201; misconceptions, 109–114; nature of, 26–27; owner draw size, 125–126; passion for work, 7–8, 111–112, 126–128, 190, 195–197, 200, 201; providing quality service, 6–7, 22–23, 55–59, 110–119; real estate investment, 75–76, 96, 97, 109, 131–133, 173–174; something for nothing, 54–55, 60–61, 64–67, 109, 116–119, 189–190, 191, 204–207, 208–209; steady job *versus* entrepreneurship, 192–193; stock market investment, 10–11, 60–62, 64, 131, 151–152, 166; straight commission, 5, 15, 23; through entrepreneurship, 119–125; time spent studying investments, 133–134

income inequality, 211–212, 219–220

income stream protection, 182–183

increasing returns, law of, 228–229

index funds, 60–62, 74, 133, 167, 178

individual responsibility, 211–214, 219–220

inflation, 109, 168–169, 208

inside information, 169

insurance, 177–180; automobile, 105, 180; disability, 178–179, 180, 183; health, 104, 208, 209; home, 105; in law of three, 104–105; life, 105, 177–178, 179; long-term care, 179–180; loss of income, 183

integrative intelligence, law of, 16

intellectual property law, 6

interest-only payments, 87

interest rates, 210–211

Internal Revenue Service (IRS), 67

inventory management, 90

investing. *see also* income generation: competition in, 133–134; law of, 27, 83, 158–160, 168, 170, 171, 173–174; for return, 60–62, 70–71, 74–76, 96–99; return on investment, 25–26, 75–76, 96–99; risk-taking, 159–160, 165–167, 175; rules for investment success, 169–171; in skill development, 11–13, 20–21, 77–81, 96–99, 219–220, 222

J

Japan, recession in, 207

Jesus Christ, 56, 161

job creation, 149, 219, 221–222

Jobs, Steve, 17, 140–141

Jordan, Michael, 22

K

knowledge workers, 6, 228–229

Krispy Kreme donuts, 229–230

Kroc, Ray, 141–142, 143

L

labor: as factor of production, 3–4; money as medium of exchange for, 1–2, 18–19

laboring jobs, 13–15, 39–40, 86

Las Vegas gambling, 10, 64–67, 189–190, 218

law of accelerating acceleration, 164–165

law of accumulation, 162–163

law of action and reaction, 34

law of attraction/magnetism, 44–55, 163–164

law of belief, 33

law of cause and effect, 5, 33–43, 157–158, 218

law of choice, 230–231
law of compounding, 12–13, 16, 30–31, 62, 160–162
law of connectivity, 225–226
law of conservation, 70–71
law of correspondence, 44–45
law of decreasing returns, 227–228
law of exchange, 1–8; defined, 1–2; earnings as measure of contribution, 4; labor as factor of production, 3–4; money as effect, not cause, 5; money as measure of value for goods and services, 2–3, 14–15, 110–119; money as medium of exchange for labor, 1–2, 18–19
law of the excluded alternative, 231
law of increasing returns, 228–229
law of integrative intelligence, 16
law of investing, 27, 83, 158–160, 168, 170, 171, 173–174
law of marginality, 226–227
law of maximization, 232–233
law of real estate, 167–169
law of repulsion, 46–48
law of scarcity, 223, 224
law of secondary consequences, 229–230, 233
law of the stock market, 165–167
law of subjective value, 231–232
law of substitution, 224–225
law of supply and demand, 21–24, 223–224
law of three, 103–105
law of unintended consequences, 230, 233
law of vibration, 46
lawsuits, 175–177
learning plans, 11–13
learning years, 62–63
LegalZoom, 180–181
Lenovo, 136
life insurance, 105, 177–178, 179
Limbaugh, Rush, 205
Lincoln, Abraham, 191

line of credit, business, 25, 91; collateral, 25, 63, 87, 91; home equity, 91
LLC (limited liability company), 185
loans. see debt management
log rolling, 205
long-term care insurance, 179–180
longtime perspective, 10–11, 30–31, 44–45, 60–62, 75–76, 166
losses, taking, 170
loss of income insurance, 183
lotteries, 10, 31, 64–67, 189, 191
Lynch, Peter, 60, 165

M

Magellan Fund, 60, 165
magic wand exercise, 201–202
Making a Lot of Money (audio program), 72
man's material welfare (MMW), 148–149
marginality, law of, 226–227
market clearing price, 227
Marx, Karl, 218
Maslow, Abraham, 194
Mastermind principle, 39
maximization, law of, 232–233
McDonald's, 118–119, 141–142, 143, 160, 220
McKinsey & Company, 120–121
Medicaid, 210
Medicare, 209, 211
Microsoft, 140–141, 142–143, 154
Millionaire Next Door, The (Stanley), 50, 62
minimum wage jobs, 22, 97, 118–119, 198–199, 220, 223–224
MLM (multilevel marketing), 102–103, 144–145
momentum principle, 162
money: as effect, not cause, 5, 55–59; as freedom, 27–28; and happiness, 187–190; as measure of value creation, 5–8; as measure of value for goods and services, 2–3, 14–15, 110–119; as measure of value placed by others, 4,

23; as medium of exchange for labor, 1–2, 18–19; myths (*see* myths about money); return on investment, 25–26, 75–76, 96–99; supply and demand for labor, 21–24

money-back guarantee, 58

mortgage debt, 95–96, 106, 131–132, 231–232

multiplying wealth. *see* wealth multiplication

mutual funds, 60–62, 74, 133, 161–162, 165, 167, 178

Myspace, 150

myths about money, 32–67; law of action and reaction, 34; law of attraction, 44–55; law of belief, 33; law of cause and effect, 33–43; lifestyles of wealthy people, 52–53, 62–64, 75; nonentrepreneur access, 60–62; something for nothing, 54–55, 60–61, 64–67, 109, 116–119, 189–190, 191, 204–207, 208–209; wealthy people think only about money, 55–59

N

national debt, 208–209

Nazis, 55

network marketing, 102–103, 144–145

New Guinea cargo cults, 8–9

Newton, Isaac, 34

Nightingale-Conant, 77–78

Nightingale, Earl, 5, 21–22, 34, 37, 56, 77, 129, 193

Nokia, 137–138

O

Obama, Barack, 98, 215

objectivity, 36–37

offshoring, 3–4, 136

online ads, 124

open-heart surgery, 110–111

optimism, 192, 195

Outliers (Gladwell), 112

outsourcing, 3–4, 136

P

Packard, Dave, 130

Parkinson's law, 26, 75

passion for work, 7–8, 111–112, 126–128, 190, 195–197, 200, 201

pension benefits, 208–209

personal guaranty, 25, 132

personal life model reinvention, 110

plunder, 54–55, 148

preemptive pay increases, 23–24, 115–116

primary consequences, 229, 233

principle of expediency, 54–55, 232–233

production lines, 57–58, 221–222

productivity, 6–7, 111–112; automation and, 221–222; contributing more value, 116–119; energy production from, 195–196; preemptive pay increases, 23–24, 115–116; providing quality service, 6–7, 22–23, 55–59, 110–119

profitability, seven-year rule for, 88–89, 125–126, 132–133, 145–146

program trading, 170

prosperity consciousness, 163

Putin, Vladimir, 55

R

raises: demands for, 22, 115–116; preemptive pay increases, 23–24, 115–116; survival bonus, 116–118; as survival bonuses, 116–118

Ramsey, Dave, 93, 99–101

Rand, Ayn, 55, 148

real estate. *see also* homes: income generation from, 75–76, 96, 97, 109, 131–133, 173–174; law of investing, 27, 158–160, 168, 170, 171, 173–174; law of real estate, 167–169; return on investment, 75–76, 96, 97; walk-on-water syndrome, 173–174

reappraisal, 170

recessions, 63, 142–143, 207, 231–232

INDEX

relationships; estate planning, 180–182; law of correspondence, 45; magic wand exercise, 201; money problems, 19; outgrowing other people, 200; results orientation in, 15; service in, 56; sympathetic resonance, 46

repulsion, law of, 46–48

resentment, 38–39, 43, 47, 188

resilience, 199–200

results orientation, 6–7, 14–15, 17–18

reticular activating system, 49–54

retirement, 26, 31, 60–61, 62–63, 72. *see also* financial freedom/independence; deferred compensation plans, 60, 99, 208–209; government pension benefits, 208–209

return on investment, 25–26, education, 96–99; real estate, 75–76, 96, 97

reverse connectivity, 225–226

revolutions, 212

right livelihood, 7–8, 111–112, 126–128, 190, 195–197, 200, 201

Riley, Pat, 17

risk-taking; calculated risks, 66; investment, 159–160, 165–167, 175; wealth creation, 140–143, 149–153

robber barons, 29–30

Rockefeller, John D., 29–30, 57

Rohn, Jim, 71

role models, 28–30

Roth IRAs, 60

Rothschild family, 29

rule of 72, 161

Russia, 55

S

sales and selling, 14–15, 40, 41–42, 52, 86–88; consignment sales, 102–103, 152; delegating, 130; demand for product or service, 124–128, 137–138; for entrepreneurs, 119–125, 130; fear of, 199–200; importance of, 120–122, 130; improving low sales, 120–122; law of increasing returns, 228–229;

MLM (multilevel marketing), 102–103, 144–145; network marketing, 102–103, 144–145; personal services, 114; 75% rule, 121–123

Samsung, 153

Santa Claus economics. *see* something for nothing

saving, 57, 60–62, 69–70; in capitalism, 149, 217–220, 234; cash reserves, 26, 122, 128, 171, 183; deferred compensation plans, 60, 99, 208–209; as income stream protection, 183; law of compounding, 12–13, 16, 30–31, 62, 160–162; law of three, 103–104; methods of, 60–61, 73–74, 94–95, 161–163; momentum principle, 162; rule of 72, 161; whole life insurance as, 177–178

scarcity, law of, 223, 224

scarcity mentality, 147–149

S corporation, 184, 185

Sears Roebuck, 58

secondary consequences, law of, 229–230, 233

Second World War, 8–9, 55

self-confidence, 191

self-discipline, 12, 71–72, 99–101, 195

self-doubt, 40–41, 79–81

self-esteem, 191–192

self-limiting beliefs, 39–41, 79–81

self-sabotage, 46–48

Selling to the Affluent (Stanley), 50

seniority, 117

service, 6–7, 22–23, 55–59, 110–119

75% rule, 121–123

seven-year rule for profitability, 88–89, 125–126, 132–133, 145–146

severance pay, 9, 18, 128

skill development, 20–21, 77–81, 96–99, 219–220, 222; continuous and never-ending improvement (CANEI), 153–155; continuous improvement, 7–8, 11–13, 143, 153–155

Slim, Carlos, 133–134

snowball method, 99–101

social comparison theory, 43, 188–190

Social Security, 209, 211

sole proprietorship, 184, 185

something for nothing, 54–55, 60–61, 64–67, 109, 116–119, 189–190, 191, 204–207, 208–209

Spanx, 152–153, 154

speculation, 8, 10–11, 166, 169

spending, 68–84; advice from experts, 83–84, 134, 160, 174, 180; cash flow, 27, 63, 76, 81–82, 132–133, 173–174, 182–183, 202; common mistakes, 63, 81–82; credit cards *versus* cash, 18–20, 86, 94–95; deferring big expenditures, 83; discipline in, 71–72; documenting, 73, 82–83; fear of failure, 72–73; frugality, 29–30, 57, 62, 64, 73–74, 81–82, 83–84; as habitual, 69–70; importance of cash flow, 63, 81–82; investing for return, 60–62, 70–71, 74–76, 96–99; investing in improving your skills, 11–13, 20–21, 77–81, 96–99, 219–220, 222; lifestyles of wealthy people, 52–53, 62–64, 75; longtime perspective, 75–76; saving *versus*, 57, 60–62, 69–70

Standard & Poor's 500, 167

Stanley, Thomas, 50, 193

starting a business. *see* entrepreneurship

stock market: day/flash trading, 10–11, 166; law of, 165–167; law of investing, 27, 83, 158–160, 168, 170, 171, 173–174; law of the, 165–167; longtime perspective, 10–11, 60–62, 64, 131; rules for investment success, 169–171; speculation in, 8, 10–11, 166, 169; value investing model, 10, 11, 151–152, 166

Stone, W. Clement, 41–42

straight commission, 5, 15, 23, 175–178

stroke symptoms, 146–147

student loans, 96–99

subjective value, law of, 231–232

substitution, law of, 224–225

suicide, 189

supply and demand, law of, 21–24, 223–224

survival bonus, 116–118

survival skills, 13–15

sympathetic resonance, 46

system entrepreneurship, 145–147

T

Talent is Overrated (Colvin), 112

taxes: capital gains, 171; income, 67, 147–148; policy for, 205–207, 216

team manufacturing, 57, 221

term insurance, 177–178, 179

Think and Grow Rich (Hill), 34

three, law of, 103–105

throwaway behavior, 192

time off, 195

Tocqueville, Alexis de, 211–212

transformation, 16–17

Transparency International, 216

Trust (Fukuyama), 216

trust busters, 29–30

trusts, 176–177

Twenty-First Century Selling seminar, 228–229

Two-Day DBA (Doctor of Business Administration) course, 35

Two-Day MBA course, 35

U

Ukraine, 55

Ulukaya, Hamdi, 127

unemployment, 54, 97, 160, 183, 205, 226, 229

unfunded liabilities, 209–211

unified field theory, 54–55

unintended consequences, law of, 230, 233

unions, 117, 206

United States: as anti-aristocratic, 211–212; dollar as reserve currency, 210; educational attainment, 216–217,

219–220; growth of government, 215–216; income inequality by choice, 219–220; individual responsibility and, 211–214; national debt, 208–209; political agendas, 214–215; as safe place to invest, 219; Santa Claus economics, 204–207; unfunded liabilities, 209–211

University of Chicago, 220

V

value: money as measure of contribution, 4, 14–15, 21–24; money as measure of value placed on goods and services, 2–3, 14–15, 110–119; productivity and, 116–119; providing quality service, 6–7, 22–23, 55–59, 110–119

value capture, 151

value creation, 5–8, 151

value investing model, 10, 11, 151–152, 166

value offering, 137–138

vibration, law of, 46

visualization, 52–53

W

Waitley, Denis, 72

walk-on-water syndrome, 173–174

Walmart, 58–59, 228

Walton, Sam, 59

wealth: lifestyle decisions, 52–53, 62–64, 75; mind-set that attracts, 50–53, 136–137; nature of, 26–27; thinking about adding value, 55–59, 106–107

wealth creation, 5, 135–155; business model development, 140–143; business plans, 144–145; competitive *versus* creative mind-set, 136–137; continuous and never-ending improvement (CANEI), 153–155; customer cocreation, 138–140; by employees, 60–62; goals, 143–145; hands-on management, 145–147; qualities of self-made billionaires,

143; risk-taking, 140–143, 149–153; scarcity *versus* abundance mentality, 147–149; system entrepreneurs, 145–147; value offering, 137–138

wealth multiplication, 156–171; law of accelerating acceleration, 164–165; law of cause and effect, 157–158; law of compound interest, 160–162; law of investing, 158–160; law of magnetism/attraction, 44–55, 163–164; law of real estate, 167–169; law of the stock market, 165–167; rules for investment success, 169–171

wealth protection, 172–186, *see also* saving; due diligence, 27, 83, 158–160, 168, 170, 171, 173–174; end-of-life discussions, 182; family-limited trusts, 176–177; forms of business organization, 183–186; income stream protection, 182–183; insurance (*see* insurance); lawsuits, 175–177; walk-on-water syndrome, 173–174; wills, 180–182

weight management, 44–45, 101, 103, 229–230

welfare, 233

What Is Seen and What Is Not Seen (Bastiat), 206

whole life insurance, 177–178, 179

Williams, Robin, 47

willpower, 12

wills, 180–182

World War II, 8–9, 55

Y

Yale University, 98, 150

yearning years, 62–63

Yellow Pages test, 206

Z

zero-base thinking, 170

zero-sum game, 166–167

Zuckerberg, Mark, 31, 149, 150